CIARAN CARSON

Selected Poems

Books of Poetry by Ciaran Carson

The New Estate
The Irish for No
Belfast Confetti
First Language
Opera Et Cetera
The Alexandrine Plan
The Twelfth of Never

CIARAN

SELECTED POEMS

CARSON

WAKE FOREST

UNIVERSITY

PRESS

Wake Forest University Press
This book is for sale only in
North America
Poems © Ciaran Carson
First Edition, published 2001
All rights reserved.
For permission, required to
reprint or broadcast more
than several lines, write to:
Wake Forest University Press
PO Box 7333, Winston-Salem,
NC 27109
ISBN 1-930630-02-6 (paperback)
ISBN 1-930630-03-4 (cloth)
LC Card Number 00-111853
Designed by R. Eckersley, and
set in Trinité types. Printed in
the United States of America

Contents

In memory of my parents

from *The New Estate* (1976)

An Early Bed

A bubble of damp
jaundiced the scrolled flowers
on the candy-stripe wallpaper.
To pass the time,
I counted the flawed petals,
each flecked angrily with red,
like father's face.

His voice unravelled from below
in disembodied phrases –
A child who struck his father,
he once told me, died
soon afterwards;
but the disobedient hand
would not be buried:

One white flower
in a grave of flowers, it struggled
upwards through the clay
as if to fend off judgement.
I thought of dying out of spite,
my parents' faces worn
to a threadbare lace . . .

I held my breath
and tried to sink below the surface
of myself, into somewhere else.
But my right hand stayed where it was,
the final speck of air
blossoming above my finger.
I cried because I could not die.

This evening, re-papering
my room, those early failures
came to light. Tissued layers
peeled beneath the decorating knife
like fronds of skin. Beneath,
gauzed over with old paste,
I found the yellowed flowers again.

The Holiday

At breakfast, I remembered
The mutilated sheep we found yesterday.
The pus had thickened to a sour cream
In the pink-lipped wounds;

Their fixed stare recalled
The waitress's eyes, the frivelled lids
Stilled bleared with sleep, the net
Of veins running through the white.

The clouds beyond the window
Curdled suddenly; a whey-coloured skin
Had crawled and wrinkled
On the coffee. Going home to Belfast

We would find a house denied our presence,
The door-handle cobwebbed –
The papers lying, unread, in the hall,
The milk turned sour upon our doorstep.

The Car Cemetery

On winter nights
The cars bring in snow from the hills,
Their bonnets white
Above a wide cold smile of chromium.

From miles away
I see you coming in, a distant star
Gone out of line, swaying
Down from the road to take the thin lane

Towards the house,
Till my warm light and your cold are married,
Your solitary noise
Is lost among the rushing of the wind.

All around the world
There is a graveyard of defunct bodies,
Wide smiles curled
In sleep. The cars at every door are hushed

Beneath a soft corrosion –
Robed in white, these brides of silence
Whose heaven
Is like ours, a detritus of lights.

To A Married Sister

Helping you to move in, unpacking,
I was proudly shown the bedroom. Patches
Of damp stained the walls a tea colour,
Like the sluggish tints of an old map.
Our mother would have said, 'A new bride
And a through-other house make a bad match'.

But you like dilapidation, the touch
Of somewhere that's been lived-in – the gloom
Of empty hallways, the shadow of the fanlight
Fading dimly, imperceptibly
Along the flowered paper; the hairline net
Of cracks on worn enamel; a tree-darkened room.

I left you cluttered with gifts – crockery,
Knives, the bed-linen still in its cellophane –
Watching you in that obscure privacy
Pick your way through the white delph
And golden straw to trace your new initials
On the spidered windowpane.

Your husband had talked of mending
Broken doors, the cheap furniture
That bore the accidents of others' lives,
That were there before you. A gold resin
Leaked from the slackened joints.
His new saw glittered like your wedding silver.

Soot

It was autumn. First, she shrouded
The furniture, then rolled back the carpet
As if for dancing; then moved
The ornaments from the mantelpiece,
Afraid his roughness might disturb
Their staid fragility.

He came; shyly, she let him in,
Feeling ill-at-ease in the newly-spacious
Room, her footsteps sounding hollow
On the boards. She watched him kneel
Before the hearth, and said something
About the weather. He did not answer,

Too busy with his work for speech.
The stem of yellow cane creaked upwards
Tentatively. After a while, he asked
Her to go outside and look, and there,
Above the roof, she saw the frayed sunflower
Bloom triumphantly. She came back

And asked how much she owed him, grimacing
As she put the money in his soiled hand.
When he had gone, a weightless hush
Lingered in the house for days. Slowly,
It settled; the fire burned cleanly;
Everything was spotless.

Hearing that soot was good for the soil,
She threw it on the flowerbeds. She would watch
It crumble, dissolving in the rain,
Finding its way to lightless crevices,
Sleeping, till in spring it would emerge softly
As the ink-bruise in the pansy's heart.

The New Estate

Forget the corncrake's elegy. Rusty
Iambics that escaped your discipline
Of shorn lawns, it is sustained by nature.
It does not grieve for you, nor for itself.
You remember the rolled gold of cornfields,
Their rustling of tinsel in the wind,
A whole field quivering like blown silk?

A shiver now runs through the laurel hedge,
And washing flutters like the swaying lines
Of a new verse. The high fidelity
Music of the newly-wed obscures your
Dedication to a life of loving
Money. What could they be for, those marble
Toilet fixtures, the silence of water-beds,
That book of poems you bought yesterday?

from The Irish for No (1987)

Dresden

Horse Boyle was called Horse Boyle because of his brother Mule;
Though why Mule was called Mule is anybody's guess. I stayed
    there once,
Or rather, I nearly stayed there once. But that's another story.
At any rate they lived in this decrepit caravan, not two miles out
    of Carrick,
Encroached upon by baroque pyramids of empty baked bean tins,
    rusts
And ochres, hints of autumn merging into twilight. Horse
    believed
They were as good as a watchdog, and to tell you the truth
You couldn't go near the place without something falling over:
A minor avalanche would ensue – more like a shop bell, really,

The old-fashioned ones on string, connected to the latch, I think,
And as you entered in, the bell would tinkle in the empty shop,
    a musk
Of soap and turf and sweets would hit you from the gloom.
    Tobacco.
Baling wire. Twine. And, of course, shelves and pyramids of tins.
An old woman would appear from the back – there was a sizzling
    pan in there,
Somewhere, a whiff of eggs and bacon – and ask you what you
    wanted;
Or rather, she wouldn't ask; she would talk about the weather.
    It had rained
That day, but it was looking better. They had just put in the
    spuds.
I had only come to pass the time of day, so I bought a token
    packet of Gold Leaf.

All this time the fry was frying away. Maybe she'd a daughter in
    there
Somewhere, though I hadn't heard the neighbours talk of it;
    if anybody knew,
It would be Horse. Horse kept his ears to the ground.
And he was a great man for current affairs; he owned the only TV
    in the place.
Come dusk he'd set off on his rounds, to tell the whole townland
    the latest
Situation in the Middle East, a mortar bomb attack in
    Mullaghbawn –
The damn things never worked, of course – and so he'd tell the
    story
How in his young day it was very different. Take young Flynn,
    for instance,
Who was ordered to take this bus and smuggle some sticks of
    gelignite

Across the border, into Derry, when the RUC – or was it the
    RIC? –
Got wind of it. The bus was stopped, the peeler stepped on. Young
    Flynn
Took it like a man, of course: he owned up right away. He opened
    the bag
And produced the bomb, his rank and serial number. For all
    the world
Like a pound of sausages. Of course, the thing was, the peeler's bike
Had got a puncture, and he didn't know young Flynn from Adam.
    All he wanted
Was to get home for his tea. Flynn was in for seven years and
    learned to speak
The best of Irish. He had thirteen words for a cow in heat;
A word for the third thwart in a boat, the wake of a boat on the ebb
    tide.

He knew the extinct names of insects, flowers, why this place was called
    Whatever: *Carrick*, for example, was *a rock.* He was damn right there –
As the man said, *When you buy meat you buy bones, when you buy land you buy stones.*
You'd be hard put to find a square foot in the whole bloody parish
That wasn't thick with flints and pebbles. To this day he could hear the grate
And scrape as the spade struck home, for it reminded him of broken bones:
Digging a graveyard, maybe – or better still, trying to dig a reclaimed tip
Of broken delph and crockery ware – you know that sound that sets your teeth on edge
When the chalk squeaks on the blackboard, or you shovel ashes from the stove?

Master McGinty – he'd be on about McGinty then, and discipline, the capitals
Of South America, Moore's *Melodies*, the Battle of Clontarf, and
Tell me this, an educated man like you: What goes on four legs when it's young,
Two legs when it's grown up, and three legs when it's old? I'd pretend
I didn't know. McGinty's leather strap would come up then, stuffed
With threepenny bits to give it weight and sting. Of course, it never did him
Any harm: *You could take a horse to water but you couldn't make him drink.*
He himself was nearly going on to be a priest.
And many's the young cub left the school, as wise as when he came.

13

Carrowkeel was where McGinty came from – *Narrow Quarter*,
  Flynn explained –
Back before the Troubles, a place that was so mean and crabbed,
Horse would have it, men were known to eat their dinner from a
  drawer.
Which they'd slide shut the minute you'd walk in.
He'd demonstrate this at the kitchen table, hunched and furtive,
  squinting
Out the window – past the teetering minarets of rust, down the
  hedge-dark aisle –
To where a stranger might appear, a passer-by, or what was
  maybe worse,
Someone he knew. Someone who wanted something. Someone
  who was hungry.
Of course who should come tottering up the lane that instant
  but his brother

Mule. I forgot to mention they were twins. They were as like
  two –
No, not peas in a pod, for this is not the time nor the place to go
  into
Comparisons, and this is really Horse's story, Horse who – now
  I'm getting
Round to it – flew over Dresden in the war. He'd emigrated first,
  to
Manchester. Something to do with scrap – redundant mill
  machinery,
Giant flywheels, broken looms that would, eventually, be ships,
  or aeroplanes.
He said he wore his fingers to the bone.
And so, on impulse, he had joined the RAF. He became a rear
  gunner.
Of all the missions, Dresden broke his heart. It reminded him of
  china.

14

As he remembered it, long afterwards, he could hear, or almost
　　hear
Between the rapid desultory thunderclaps, a thousand tinkling
　　echoes –
All across the map of Dresden, store-rooms full of china shivered,
　　teetered
And collapsed, an avalanche of porcelain, slushing and cascading:
　　cherubs,
Shepherdesses, figurines of Hope and Peace and Victory, delicate
　　bone fragments.
He recalled in particular a figure from his childhood, a milkmaid
Standing on the mantelpiece. Each night as they knelt down for
　　the rosary,
His eyes would wander up to where she seemed to beckon to him,
　　smiling,
Offering him, eternally, her pitcher of milk, her mouth of rose
　　and cream.

One day, reaching up to hold her yet again, his fingers stumbled,
　　and she fell.
He lifted down a biscuit tin, and opened it.
It breathed an antique incense: things like pencils, snuff, tobacco.
His war medals. A broken rosary. And there, the milkmaid's
　　creamy hand, the outstretched
Pitcher of milk, all that survived. Outside, there was a scraping
And a tittering; I knew Mule's step by now, his careful drunken
　　weaving
Through the tin-stacks. I might have stayed the night, but
　　there's no time
To go back to that now; I could hardly, at any rate, pick up the
　　thread.
I wandered out through the steeples of rust, the gate that was a
　　broken bed.

Judgement

The tarred road simmered in a blue haze. The reservoir was dry.
The railway sleepers oozed with creosote. Not a cloud to be seen in the sky

We were sitting at the Camlough halt – Johnny Mickey and
    myself – waiting
For a train that never seemed to come. He was telling me this story
Of a Father Clarke, who wanted to do in his dog. A black and white
    terrier.
He says to the servant boy, *Take out that old bitch, he says, and drown*
    her.
Johnny Mickey said the servant boy was Quigley, and now that he
    remembered it,
He'd been arrested by a Sergeant Flynn, for having no bell on his
    bike.
Hardly a hanging crime, you might say. But he was fined fifteen
    shillings.

The prisoner left the court-room and his step was long and slow
By day and night he did contrive to fill this sergeant's heart with woe

So there was this auction one day, and Quigley sneaks in the back.
A lot of crockery ware came up. Delph bowls. Willow-pattern.
    Chamberpots.
The bidding started at a shilling. Quigley lifts his finger. One-and-
    six.
Everyone pretending not to look at one another. Or to know each
    other.
Nods and winks. A folded *Dundalk Democrat*. Spectacles put on and
    off.
And so on, till he won the bid at fifteen shillings. *Name, please,*
Says the auctioneer. *Sergeant Flynn, says Quigley, Forkhill Barracks.*

For to uphold the letter of the law this sergeant was too willing
I took the law upon myself and fined him back his fifteen shillings

He rambled on a bit – how this Flynn's people on his mother's
   side
Were McErleans from County Derry, how you could never trust
A McErlean. When they hanged young McCorley on the bridge of
   Toome
It was a McErlean who set the whole thing up. That was in '98,
But some things never changed. You could trust a dog but not a
   cat.
It was something in their nature, and nature, as they say, will
   out.
The pot would always call the kettle black. He hummed a few
   lines.

Come tender-hearted Christians all attention pay to me
Till I relate and communicate these verses two or three
Concerning of a gallant youth was cut off in his bloom
And died upon the gallows tree near to the town of Toome

Which brought Johnny Mickey back to the priest and the terrier
   bitch.
Quigley, it transpired, had walked the country – Ballinliss and
   Aughaduff,
Slievenacapall, Carnavaddy – looking for a place to drown her.
It was the hottest summer in living memory. Not a cloud to be
   seen in the sky.
The Cully Water was a trickle. The Tullyallen and the
   Ummeracam were dry.
Not a breath of wind. Not so much water as would drown a rat.
   After three days
Quigley and the bitch came back. They were both half-dead with
   thirst.

He looked her up he looked her down in his heart was ne'er a pang
I'll tell you what says Father Clarke if she won't be drowned she'll hang

Johnny Mickey said that priests had a great way with ropes and
  knots.
It was one of the tricks that they learned in the seminary.
  Something to do
With chasubles and albs. In less time than it takes to tell, Father
  Flynn
Had rigged up a noose. They brought the bitch out to the orchard
And strung her up from the crook of an apple tree. And who was
  passing by
But the poet McCooey. He peeped through a hole in the hedge.
He spotted the two boys at their trade, and this is what he said:

A man with no bell on his bike a man with a single bed
It's hardly any wonder that you'd go off your head
Poor old bitch door old friend you died without a bark
Sentenced by Johnny Quigley and hung by Father Clarke

Of course, said Johnny Mickey, your man McCooey's long since
  dead.
A white plume of steam appeared around the bend. A long
  lonesome blast.
The tracks began to shimmer and to hum. Our train was coming
  in
And not a minute late. It shivered to a halt. We both got on.
We would pass the crazy map of a dried-up reservoir. A water-
  tower.
We would watch the telegraph lines float up and down, till we
  arrived
At the other end; I would hand Mickey Quigley over to the two
  attendants.

Farewell unto you sweet Drumaul if in you I had stayed
Among the Presbyterians I ne'er would have been betrayed
The gallows tree I ne'er would have seen had I remained there
For Dufferin you betrayed me McErlean you set the snare

Calvin Klein's Obsession

I raised my glass, and – solid, pungent, like the soot-encrusted
    brickwork
Of the Ulster Brewery – a smell of yeast and hops and malt swam
    up:
I sniff and sniff again, and try to think of what it is I am remembering:
I think that's how it goes, like Andy Warhol's calendar of
    perfumes,
Dribs and drabs left over to remind him of that season's smell.
Very personal, of course, as *Blue Grass* is for me the texture of a fur
Worn by this certain girl I haven't seen in years. Every time that
    Blue Grass
Hits me, it is 1968. I'm walking with her through the smoggy
    early dusk
Of West Belfast: coal-smoke, hops, fur, the smell of stout and
    whiskey
Breathing out from somewhere. So it all comes back, or nearly all,
A long-forgotten kiss.

Never quite. Horses' dung is smoking on the cobbles.
    Cobblestones?
I must have gone back further than I thought, to brewers' drays
    and milk-carts,
Brylcreem, *Phoenix* beer. Or candy apples – rich hard dark-brown
    glaze
Impossible to bite at first, until you licked and licked and sucked
    a way

Into the soft core. A dark interior, where I'd also buy a twist of
    snuff
For my grandma. She'd put two pinches on a freckled fist, and sniff.
Then a sip of whiskey, and, as always, *I'm not long for this world.*
My father would make a face: *a whingeing gate,* he'd say, *hangs
    longest –*
Hoping it was true, perhaps – a phrase he'd said so often, he'd
    forgotten
When he said it last. That *Gold Label* whiskey – nearly like a
    perfume:
I go crazy because I want to smell them all so much,

Warhol's high-pitched New York whine comes on again, with
All those exhalations of the 'thirties and the 'forties: Guerlain's
Sous le Vent, Saravel's *White Christmas,* Corday's *Voyage à Paris,* or
Kathleen Mary Quinlan's *Rhythm:* bottles of bottle-green, bruise-
    blues
Darker than the pansies at the cemetery gate-lodge, bottles of
    frosted glass
And palest lilac – *l'odeur de ton sein chaleureux* – a rush of musk
And incense, camphor, beckons from the back of the wardrobe; I'd
    slipped
Through the mirror in a dream. *Opium* by Yves St Laurent? More
    than likely,
What my mother used to call a guilty conscience, or something
    that I ate:
Cheese and chopped dill pickle on wheaten farls, looking, if I
    thought of it,
Like Boots' *Buttermilk and Clover* soap –

Slipping and slipping from my grasp, clunking softly downwards
    through
The greying water; I have drowsed off into something else. The
    ornate fish

And frog and water-lily motif on the bathroom wallpaper reminds
    me
How in fact I'd stripped it off some months ago. It was April, a time
Of fits and starts; fresh leaves blustered at the window, strips and
    fronds
Of fish and water-lilies sloughed off round my feet. A Frank Ifield
    song
From 1963, I think, kept coming back to me: *I remember you – you're
    the one*
Who made my dreams come true – just a few – kisses ago. I'm taking
One step forward, two steps back, trying to establish what it was
    about her
That made me fall in love with her, if that's what it was; *infatuation*
Was a vogue word then –

It meant it wasn't all quite real. Like looking at my derelict back
    garden,
Its scraggy ranks of docks and nettles, thistles, but thinking
There was something else, flicking idly through the pages of a
    catalogue:
Flowered violets and whites, or grey and silver foliage, suggesting
Thunderclouds and snowstorms, rivers, fountains; artemesias and
    lilies,
Phlox, gentians, scillas, snowdrops, crocuses; and thymes and
    camomiles
Erupted from the paving-cracks, billowing from half-forgotten
    corners;
An avalanche of jasmine and wisteria broke through. Or, the
    perfume
Of *Blue Grass*, bittersweet, which is, just at this moment, just a
    memory.
How often did she wear it, anyway? I must look her up again some
    day.
And can it still be bought?

For there are memories that have no name; you don't know what to
    ask for.
The merest touch of sunshine, a sudden breeze, might summon up
A corner of your life you'd thought, till then, you'd never occupied.
Her mother, for example, owned this second-hand shop, which is
    where
The fur coat came from, anonymous with shades of someone else.
    Rummaging
Through piles of coats and dresses, I'd come across a thing that
    until then
I'd never wanted: a white linen 'fifties jacket with no back vent,
Just that bit out of fashion, it was fashionable, or maybe, as they
    say,
It was just the thing I had been looking for. So, a box of worn shoes
Might bring me back to 1952, teetering across the kitchen floor
In my mother's high heels –

Not that I wanted to be her; easing off the lid of her powder
    compact,
Breathing in the flesh-coloured dust, was just a way of feeling her
    presence.
And so I have this image of an assignation, where it all comes back,
Or nearly all, a long-forgotten kiss: subdued lighting, musak – no,
    a live
Piano – tinkling in its endless loop; there is candlelight and
    Cointreau,
Whispered nothings, as Kathleen Mary Quinlan's Rhythm meets,
    across
A discreet table, Calvin Klein's Obsession. He has prospered since
He saw her last. There is talk of all the years that separated them,
    whatever
Separated them at first. There is talk of money, phrased as talk of
Something else, of how there are some things that can't be bought.
Or maybe it's the name you buy, and not the thing itself.

Whatever Sleep It Is

The leg was giving me a problem, interfering, somehow, with the
total
Composition – I didn't know, at this stage, if he'd be a walker or a
skier.
Certainly, a far-away look in his eyes suggested mountain scenery,
the light
Falling gradually, then pouring as an avalanche across a great
divide:
Cuckoo-clocks and cow-bells, everything as full of holes as a Swiss
cheese.
And I wanted to give him a leather jacket – leather is 'interesting'
though
Sometimes it's easy and sometimes not, depending on the time of
day, the light,
The consistency of this particular tube of burnt sienna. So if it
doesn't work
It might be tweed. But then the air of mystery might vanish, this
spy
Or pilot whose whereabouts have yet to be established –

At any rate, I painted out the leg, and put in this flight of stairs
instead.
It seemed to me it should lead to a skylight, so dusty as to be
opaque,
Cobwebbed, opening with a slow reluctant creak – the see-saw of a
donkey –
On to clouds and bits of sky. A gusty March day, maybe, with a
touch of rain
Ticking on the glass. Someone keeps asking me why I hold my
hand like that,
But it's not to keep off the light – it's more to do with how you
often

Don't remember what a hand looks like. So you paint your own,
    and give it
To this character who might, indeed, be you, but with a life you
    haven't
Worked out yet. The sleeve of your jacket ticked with sky-blue,
    Chinese white.
I think the story is starting to take shape:

It usually takes three days, four days, and you can reckon on a week
Before it's finished. On the seventh day I'd go out on the town and
    celebrate,
And then come back and look at it again: sometimes I'd say yes,
    sometimes no.
On day five, for instance, the skylight acquired a broken pane, and
    someone
Had to be responsible: I thought of a message wrapped around a
    stone.
What was being said, and why? Could it be that the character I'd
    painted out
By now was lurking out there? Perhaps he is in love with this girl
Hunched in the attic, where the light-source now becomes a
    candle
Stuck in a Chianti bottle, a love that tells itself by paper, stone,
    scissors.
And the donkey keeps coming back,

Its too-big head lolling over a five-barred gate that opens out on to
An orchard: there is, in fact, a bowl of apples at her elbow that she
    seems
To be ignoring. It is there to concentrate the light, I think – flecks
And smuts of amber, yellow, russet, green, each fruit swirled into a
    fist,
The navel clenched between the finger and the thumb. Meanwhile
    Mr Natural,

As we'll call him, has climbed on to the roof, and, with his feet lodged

In the guttering, is staring through the hole at her. *The pane of glass*

I skimmed this morning from the drinking-trough, he whispers to himself,

Melted, and I let it fall and break. Early frost: the stars are blazing

Now like snowflakes – stem end and blossom end

Swelling and dimming over the black Alp of the roof. It is an October

Sort of March, the apples ripened out of season; and now that the ink-dark sky

Lightens into sapphire, I see it is an angel, not a man, who has

Descended, looking faintly puzzled at the poor response of the girl

To whatever important announcement he has just made. She is, in fact, asleep,

Oblivious also to the clink and hum of the electric milk float

Which has just pulled up outside. And the milkman looks up, momentarily

Amazed at curtains, wings, gusting from the attic window. He rubs his eyes;

He is still drowsy with these six days out of seven. Tomorrow yawns ahead

With routine promises; tomorrow, after all, he will be free.

Belfast Confetti

Suddenly as the riot squad moved in, it was raining exclamation marks,

Nuts, bolts, nails, car-keys. A fount of broken type. And the explosion

Itself – an asterisk on the map. This hyphenated line, a burst of
    rapid fire . . .
I was trying to complete a sentence in my head, but it kept
    stuttering,
All the alleyways and side-streets blocked with stops and colons.

I know this labyrinth so well – Balaclava, Raglan, Inkerman,
    Odessa Street –
Why can't I escape? Every move is punctuated. Crimea Street.
    Dead end again.
A Saracen, Kremlin-2 mesh. Makrolon face-shields. Walkie-
    talkies. What is
My name? Where am I coming from? Where am I going? A
    fusillade of question-marks.

August 1969

As the huge façade of Greeves's Mill is washed in a Niagara of
    flame
The riot fizzles out. Still smouldering as the troops march in, this
    welcome,
Singing, dancing on the streets. Confetti drifts across the city:
Charred receipts and bills-of-lading, contracts, dockets, pay-slips.
The weave is set: a melt of bobbins, spindles, shuttles.

Happy days, my mother claims, the mill-girls chattering, linking
    arms.
But then, it all changed when I met your father. The flicker of a smile.
It lights again on this creased photograph, a weekend
    honeymoon.
She is crossing the Liffey, the indelible ink of Dublin September
    1944.

Campaign

They had questioned him for hours. Who exactly was he? And
    when
He told them, they questioned him again. When they accepted
    who he was, as
Someone not involved, they pulled out his fingernails. Then
They took him to a waste-ground somewhere near the Horseshoe
    Bend, and told him
What he was. They shot him nine times.

A dark umbilicus of smoke was rising from a heap of burning
    tyres.
The bad smell he smelt was the smell of himself. Broken glass
    and knotted Durex.
The knuckles of a face in a nylon stocking. I used to see him in
    the Gladstone Bar,
Drawing pints for strangers, his almost perfect fingers flecked
    with scum.

Slate Street School

Back again. Day One. Fingers blue with cold. I joined the
    lengthening queue.
Roll call. Then inside: chalk dust and iced milk, the smell of
    watered ink.
Roods, perches, acres, ounces, pounds, tons weighed
    imponderably in the darkening
Air. We had chanted the twelve-times table for the twelfth or
    thirteenth time
When it began to snow. Chalky numerals shimmered down; we
    crowded to the window –

These are the countless souls of purgatory, whose numbers constantly
   diminish
And increase; each flake as it brushes to the ground is yet another soul
   released.
And I am the avenging Archangel, stooping over mills and
   factories and barracks.
I will bury the dark city of Belfast forever under snow: inches, feet,
   yards, chains, miles.

Asylum

The first indication was this repeated tic, the latch jigging and
   clicking
As he rehearsed the possibility of entering, or opening. Maybe
It was a knock, a question; Uncle John was not all there. Yet he had
His father's eyes, his mother's nose; and I myself, according to my
   mother,
Had his mouth. I would imagine speaking for him sometimes. He
   had
A second cousin's hands, or a cousin's twice removed, an uncle's
   way of walking:
In other words, he was himself. So he might walk in this very
   minute, or turn
His back on us to contemplate the yellow brick edgings of the
   bricked-in
Windows of the mill wall opposite. He seemed to see things that
   we didn't
See: cloud-shadow eddying and swirling round a manhole; the bits
   of grit
That glittered at the edges; individual as dirt, the dog-leg walk of a
   dog
As it followed its nose from one side of the street to the other. His
   ears

Might prick to the clatter of an empty tin kicked down an entry,
Diminishing the yelps of children as their skipping rope became
    a blur,
Then slowed and stopped, then whipped back up again, the up-
    hill down-dale
Quickening pulse of a cardiograph. We watched him hover and
    dilate
In the frosted glass. Someone would get up; he would retreat. An
    electric
Yellow bakery van hummed by; he sniffed the air. A car backfired.

Like the fast-forward or the rewind button, everything is going
    far too
Fast, though we might know precisely, having heard it all before
    for real,
What is going on, like that climactic moment of a rounded,
    oratorical
Gesture, practised in the mirror till it seemed completely
    unfamiliar:
The hyped-up, ninety-to-the-dozen commentary that illustrates,
    in retrospect,
The split second when a goal is scored; the laid back, bit-by-bit
    analysis
As we take in every slowed down motion of the replay. We are
    looking
For a piece we know is there, amongst the clutter and the plug of
    bottles,
Whispering, the chink of loose change, the unfamiliar voices that
    are us
And cloud our hearing. The repeated melancholic parp of a car-
    horn
Eventually has heralded the moment: now we know what's
    coming next, the voice

Hoarsened by the second-generation tape, the echo of a nearly
     empty dusty
Concert hall, illuminated, we imagine, by the voice, one shaft of
     fitful sunlight
That retreated almost instantly to a nimbo-cumulus – gold-
     edged, slate-blue,
Glimmering between its cup and lip – imponderably weighing
     on the skylight.
A yellow bakery van hums by. There is a lull, and then a car
     backfires.

It's getting nearer now, that out-of-focus look he had: a wall-eye
With its yellowed white, the confused rainbow of the iris
     weeping unpredictably.
The tortoise-shell frame had one missing lens. Why they were bi-
     focals
I don't know; he didn't read. Spinning yarns was more his line,
     always something
Off the top of his head. Or he might sing a song: perhaps *I'm
     going down the town
And I know who's going with me. I have a wee boy of my own, and his
     name is –*
Here he'd mention my name, which was almost my name; half of
     it, at least,
Was right. All this while he champed, between gulps of tea, two
     thick buttered
Doorsteps of a *Peter Pan* loaf, and cast his eye on the yellowed
     pages
Of an *Old Moore's Almanac* for 1948, the year, in fact, that I was
     born.
Storms this month, I see; hurricanes and thunder . . . the almanac was
     upside down,
But sure enough, just then, above the smoke-stack of the mill on
     up the street,

30

I caught a dark umbilicus of cloud, a momentary flash. Rain
    pattered on the window.
A yellow bakery van went by; he sniffed the ozone. A car backfired.

You can tell that this was all some time ago, although it does
    repeat itself.
On this particular day, my other uncle, Pat, had just come in from
    work.
He plunked two loaves down on the table. A doughy-sour
    inveterate smell
Breathed out from him, and as he lifted off the white cloud of his
    cap, it sparked off
The authoritative onset of this other, needle-in-the-haystack day
    that I
Began with. That ratchety delay with which the clock is poised
    conjugating
All its tensed-up coils and springs: rain pattered on the window.
    An electric
Yellow bakery van whirred off. A car backfired. Someone seemed to
    get up very
Slowly. A dog was barking. The car backfired again. Everything
    was getting faster

And the door bursts open. He is babbling, stammering,
    contractions
Getting nearer, nearer, all the blips run into one another till they
    are
A wave, a wall: *They said to push, she pushed, they said to shut her
    mouth,*
She pushed, they said to keep her head down, and she pushed once more –
The wave has almost broken – *more, they said:* a lock of hair, a bald
    patch,
Hair again. Flecks of blood and foam. He cannot get it all out fast
    enough.

Afterwards, a lull. He sits up and he takes a cup of tea, a slice of
toast.
He is himself again, though I can see myself in him. *I remember very
well,* he says,
When you were born; oh yes, thunder, hurricanes; and as I see the
bruised
Posthumous violet of his face, I hear him talk about the shape of
this particular
Cloud he saw last week, or this dog he'd noticed last week, which
he'd imitate,
Panting, slabbering and heaving as it lolled about the margins of
the new estate –
Nettles, yellow chickweed, piss-the-beds – sniffing, wagging,
following itself
Back through that remembered day of complex perfume, a trail of
moments
Dislocated, then located. This dog. That bitch. There is a long-
forgotten
Whimper, a groan of joy as it discovers home: a creosoted hutch, a
bowl,
The acrid spoor of something that was human.

from *Belfast Confetti* (1989)

Loaf

I chewed it over, this whiff I got just now, but trying to pin down
That aroma – yeast, salt, flour, water – is like writing on the waxed
    sleeve
That it's wrapped in: the nib keeps skidding off. Or the ink won't
    take. Blue-black
Quink is what I used then. I liked the in-between-ness of it, neither
One thing nor the other. A *Conway Stewart* fountain pen, blue-ish
    green
Mock tortoiseshell . . . the lever sticking sometimes in the quick of
    my thumb,
I'd fill her up: a contented slurp like the bread you use to sup up
Soup. McWatters' pan loaf, some said, was like blotting-paper: I
    thought of
Leonardo's diary, or a mirror code ending with, *Eat this.*
Well, some people *like* blotting-paper. I used to eat chalk self. Raw
Flour, oatmeal. Paper. A vitamin deficiency? The corners of
My books weren't dog-eared, they were chewed. But neatly
    chewed, like the thumb-index
Of a dictionary. I ate my way from A to Z, the list of weights
And measures. So now I'm in McWatters' flour-loft. Grains, pecks
    and bushels:

So much raw material. I was raw. This was a summer job, not real
Work. Myself and this other skiver, we mostly talked of this and
    that –
Cigarettes and whiskey – between whatever it was we were
    supposed
To do. Joe reckoned that Jameson's *Three Swallows* was hard to beat
Though you could make a case for their *Robin Redbreast* or Power's
    Gold Label.
One had the edge the others didn't, though you couldn't quite
    describe it.

Like Gallaher's *Greens*: dry, smoky, biting. He had this bebop
    hairstyle –
Bee-bap, as they say in Belfast, a golden fuzz pricked up from the
    scalp –
And he'd done time at one time or another for some petty crime.
    Theft?
Jiggery-pokery. Night-shifts. The kind of fly moves that get you
    caught.
And as it happened, he was between times just then, like me
    between terms.

It seemed the Health Inspectors were due in a while, so we were
    given
Galvanized buckets, sponges, those mops with the head of an
    albino
Golliwog. The place breathed gunge and grease, the steamy damp
    of baking bread.
So as I say, we talked: football, drink, girls, horses, though I didn't
    know
Much on any of these scores. They were clouds on the blue of the
    future.
Walking the slippery catwalk from one bake-room to the next –
    like Dante's
Inferno, the midnight glare of ovens, a repeated doughy slap
Of moulds being filled – we'd think of the cool of the loo or a
    lunchtime pint.
The bitter edge of Guinness would cut through the bread and
    oxtail soup
Till bread and soup and stout became all one. We would talk with
    our mouths full.

Then back to *Ajax* and *Domestos*, the Augean pandemonium.
Or sorting out spoiled loaves for pig-feed – waxed wrappers in
    one bag, sliced pan

In the other; the pigs, it seemed, were particular. At other times,
Stacking up empty flour-sacks: cloudy caesurae floating one on
      top
Of one another, the print so faded we could barely read the text;
That choked-up weave meant nothing much but passing time.
      Expanding moments,
Watching dough rise, the stretch-marks lost in the enormous
      puffball – Is this
The snow that was so bright last year?
We worked slowly through the levels, till
We found ourselves at last in No. 2 loft, high above the racket.
My last week. As for him, he didn't know. Muffled by forgotten
      drifts
Of flour, I was thinking of the future, he was buried in the past.
This move he'd worked, this girl he'd known. Everything stored
      away in cells.
Pent-up honey talk oozed out of him, while I sang, *Que sera sera.*

He asked if I'd remember him. We wrote our names on the
      snowed-up panes.
The date, the names of girls, hearts and arrows. We made up
      affairs between
The bakers and the packers – bread and paper – then we wiped it
      all clean.
The glass shone for the first time in years. We were staring out
      the window
At the end of summer. Aeroplanes flew by at intervals, going
      elsewhere:
Tiny specks, the white lines of their past already fuzzing up the
      blue.

Snow

A white dot flicked back and forth across the bay window: not
A table-tennis ball, but 'ping-pong', since this is happening in
        another era,
The extended leaves of the dining table – scratched mahogany
        veneer –
Suggesting many such encounters, or time passing: the celluloid
        diminuendo
As it bounces off into a corner and ticks to an incorrigible stop.
I pick it up days later, trying to get that pallor right: it's neither
        ivory
Nor milk. Chalk is better; and there's a hint of pearl, translucent
Lurking just behind opaque. I broke open the husk so many
        times
And always found it empty; the pith was a wordless bubble.

Though there's nothing in the thing itself, bits of it come back
        unbidden,
Playing in the archaic dusk till the white blip became invisible.
Just as, the other day, I felt the tacky pimples of a ping-pong bat
When the bank-clerk counted out my money with her rubber
        thimble, and knew
The black was bleeding into red. Her face was snow and roses just
        behind

The bullet-proof glass: I couldn't touch her if I tried. I crumpled up
    the chit –
No use in keeping what you haven't got – and took a stroll to Ross's
    auction.
There was this Thirties scuffed leather sofa I wanted to make a bid
    for.
Gestures, prices: soundlessly collateral in the murmuring room.

I won't say what I paid for it: anything's too much when you have
    nothing.
But in the dark recesses underneath the cushions I found myself
    kneeling
As decades of the Rosary dragged by, the slack of years ago hauled
    up
Bead by bead; and with them, all the haberdashery of loss – cuff
    buttons,
Broken ball-point pens and fluff, old pennies, pins and needles, and
    yes,
A ping-pong ball. I cupped it in my hands like a crystal, seeing not
The future, but a shadowed parlour just before the blinds are
    drawn. Someone
Has put up two trestles. Handshakes all round, nods and whispers.
Roses are brought in, and suddenly, white confetti seethes against
    the window.

Eleven horsemen –
Not one of them turns his head –
Through the wind-blown snow.
                — Shiki

Ambition

'I did not allow myself to think of ultimate escape . . .
one step at a time was enough.'
— John Buchan, Mr Standfast

Now I've climbed this far, it's time to look back. But smoke
    obscures
The panorama from the Mountain Loney spring. The city and the
    mountain are on fire.
My mouth's still stinging from the cold sharp shock of water - a
    winter taste
In summer - but my father's wandered off somewhere. I can't
    seem to find him.
We'd been smoking 'coffin nails', and he'd been talking of his
    time inside, how
Matches were that scarce, you'd have to split them four ways
    with your thumb-nail;
And seven cigarette ends made a cigarette. *Keep a thing for seven*
    years,
You'll always find a use for it, he follows in the same breath . . . it
    reminds me
Of the saint who, when he had his head cut off, picked up his
    head, and walked
With it for seven miles. And the wise man said, *The distance doesn't*
    matter,
It's the first step that was difficult.

Any journey's like that - *the first step of your life,* my father
    interrupts -
Though often you take one step forward, two steps back. For if
    time is a road,
It's fraught with ramps and dog-legs, switchbacks and spaghetti;
    here and there,

The dual carriageway becomes a one-track, backward mind. And
    bits of the landscape
Keep recurring: it seems as if I've watched the same suburban
    tennis match
For hours, and heard, at ever less-surprising intervals, the
    applause of pigeons
Bursting from a loft. Or the issue is not yet decided, as the
    desultory handclaps
Turn to rain. The window that my nose is pressed against is
    breathed-on, giving
Everything a sfumato air. I keep drawing faces on it, or practising
    my signature.

And if time is a road, then you're checked again and again
By a mobile checkpoint. One soldier holds a gun to your head.
    Another soldier
Asks you questions, and another checks the information on the
    head computer.
Your name. Your brothers' names. Your father's name. His
    occupation. As if
The one they're looking for is not you, but it might be you. Looks
    like you
Or smells like you. And suddenly, the posthumous aroma of an
    empty canvas
Postman's sack – twine, ink, dead letters – wafts out from the
    soldiers'
Sodden khaki. It's obvious they're bored: one of them is watching
    Wimbledon
On one of those postage-stamp-sized TV screens. *Of course, the
    proper shot,*
An unseen talking head intones, *should have been the lob.* He's
    using words like
Angled, volley, smash and *strategy.* Someone is fighting a losing battle.

Isn't that the way, that someone tells you what you should have
    done, when
You've just done the opposite? *Did you give the orders for this man's
    death?*
On the contrary, the accused replies, as if he'd ordered birth or
    resurrection.
Though *one nail drives out another,* as my father says.

And my father should have known better than to tamper with
    Her Majesty's
Royal Mail – or was it His, then? His humour was to take an Irish
    ha'penny
With the harp on the flip side, and frank a letter with it. Some
    people didn't
See the joke; they'd always thought him a Republican. He was
    reported,
Laid off for a month. Which is why he never got promoted. So one
    story goes.
The other is a war-time one, where he's supposed to go to England
For a training course, but doesn't, seeing he doesn't want to get
    conscripted.
My mother's version is, he lacked ambition. He was too content to
    stay
In one place. He liked things as they were . . . *perfect touch, perfect
    timing, perfect
Accuracy:* the commentary has just nudged me back a little, as I
    manage
To take in the action replay. There's a tiny puff of chalk, as the ball
    skids off
The line, like someone might be firing in slow motion, far away:
    that otherwise
Unnoticeable faint cloud on the summer blue, which makes the
    sky around it
All the more intense and fragile.

It's nearer to a winter blue. A zig-zag track of footsteps is imprinted
On the frosted tennis-court: it looks as if the Disappeared One rose
    before
First light, and stalked from one side of the wire cage to the other,
    off
Into the glinting laurels. No armed wing has yet proclaimed
    responsibility:
One hand washes the other, says my father, *as sure as one funeral makes
    many.*
For the present is a tit-for-tat campaign, exchanging *now* for *then,*
The Christmas post of Christmas Past, the black armband of the
    temporary man;
The insignia have mourned already for this casual preserve.
    Threading
Through the early morning suburbs and the monkey-puzzle trees, a
    smell of coffee lingers,
Imprisoned in the air like wisps of orange peel in marmalade; and
    sleigh-bell music
Tinkles on the radio, like ice cubes in a summer drink. I think I'm
    starting, now,
To know the street map with my feet, just like my father.

God never shuts one door, said my father, *but he opens up another;* and
    then,
I walked the iron catwalk naked in the freezing cold: he's back into his
    time
As internee, the humiliation of the weekly bath. It was seven weeks
    before
He was released: it was his younger brother they were after all the
    time.
God never opens one door, but he shuts another: my uncle was inside for
    seven years.
At his funeral, they said how much I looked like him: I've got his
    smoker's cough,

At any rate. And now my father's told to cut down on the
    cigarettes, he smokes
Them three or four puffs at a time. Stubs them out and lights
    them, seven times.
I found him yesterday a hundred yards ahead of me, struggling,
    as the blazing
Summer hauled him one step at a time into a freezing furnace.
    And with each step
He aged. As I closed in on him, he coughed. I coughed. He
    stopped and turned,
Made two steps back towards me, and I took one step forward.

Darkness never flows
Except down by the river:
Shimmering fireflies.
                — Chiyo

Hairline Crack

It could have been or might have been. Everything Provisional
    and Sticky,
Daily splits and splinters at the drop of a hat or a principle –
The right hand wouldn't even know it was the right hand; some
    would claim it
As the left. If only this, if only that, if only pigs could fly.
Someone decides, hawk or dove. Ambushes are sprung. Velvet fist.
    Iron glove.

It was on the stroke of midnight by the luminous dial of the
    clock
When this woman, caught in crossfire, stooped for the dashboard
    cigarette lighter.
In that instant, a bullet neatly parted her permanent wave. So
    now
She tells the story, how a cigarette made all the odds. Between
    life. And death.

Bloody Hand

Your man, says the Man, *will walk into the bar like this* – here his
    fingers
Mimic a pair of legs, one stiff at the knee – *so you'll know exactly*
What to do. He sticks a finger to his head. *Pretend it's child's play* –
The hand might be a horse's mouth, a rabbit or a dog. Five
    handclaps.
Walls have ears: the shadows you throw are the shadows you try
    to throw off.

I snuffed out the candle between finger and thumb. Was it the
    left hand
Hacked off at the wrist and thrown to the shores of Ulster? Did
    Ulster
Exist? Or the Right Hand of God, saying *Stop* to this and *No* to
    that?
My thumb is the hammer of a gun. The thumb goes up. The
    thumb goes down.

The Knee

His first bullet is a present, a mark of intelligence that will
End in the gutter behind The Clock Bar, since he keeps on doing
   what
He's not supposed to. The next one is for real, what we've just
   talked about.
It seems he was a hood, whatever, or the lads were just being
   careful.
Two and two were put together; what they added up to wasn't
   five.

Visiting time: he takes his thirteen-month-old son on his other
   knee.
Learning to walk, he suddenly throws himself into the staggering
Distance between his father and his father's father, hands held
   up high,
His legs like the hands of a clock, one trying to catch up on the
   other.

I've just put on this
borrowed armour: second-hand
cold freezes my bones.
                              — Buson

46

Bed-Time Story

The sound effects were really very simple: a creaky leather wallet – here,
The speaker reached into his pocket and produced the very article –
Might stand for the marching boots of the Seven Dwarfs. Almost
    instantly,
I stepped into my father's creased, enormous shoes, their puckered
    insole ridges:
Cold, cold, so many hours until he comes back trudging through
    the snow,
The empty canvas sack around his neck; but never empty-handed –
    always promises
Of stories, or postcards left in limbo, *Not Known At This Address.* On
    the back,
You'll never guess who I met here – I'll tell you all about it when I see you.
Or bits of hairy twine come snaking out, the same gruff texture
As his navy-blue, tobacco-scented serge. The braid. The black
    mirror of his cap-peak.

And in the ink-dark celluloid, confused images of the narrative
    appear:
Disney's artists gather round like dwarfs, or ravens, as Disney,
Flaps his arms to illustrate the story. He imitates a talking bird.
His hand opens and shuts like a beak. He gets them to do the
    same, to feel
The movement, the whole body swept along in mimicry, as they
    get it down
On paper. *He seemed to make it up as he went along.* Or maybe these
    were dreams,
Rehearsed for nights until they dawned into a blue configuration
Set off by floating, regal clouds; as if, already spoken-for and
    animated,
The day proclaimed its destination, knowing what was coming
    next. The way

A flock of birds will make a fist. Which flits open, shuts again,
    then vanishes.

For the blue is the sky of an air-mail letter, the clouds are puffs of
    smoke
Which punctuate my father's story. I see his fingernail is stained
    with nicotine,
Or maybe that's a trick of the light, the yellowish burnt umber
    which precedes
A thunderstorm. He is sprawled out on the sofa, I am in the
    rowing-boat
Between his knees. A squall will figure shortly, summoned up
    from nowhere;
As this episode draws to a close, the castaway will cling to broken
    spars,
The tatters of his once-proud enterprise. By the island of
    tomorrow he will know
If he is drowned or saved; as yet, he's in the dark, treading amber
    water.
And now the time-lapsed, wind-torn envelope is swallowed in
    the cobalt night,
My father lies asleep; he's been abroad since early morning.

His hands are folded on his chest, as if fastened on a rosary.
He has gathered silence over him, like his overcoat I drape around
    me.
I feel its snowbound, dangling weight, the broad cuffs where my
    hands are lost,
The trailing hem. The regal crown of his cap. The cool damp
    headband.
I touch the shining peak. Then the coarse weave of the sack. The
    glinting buckles.
I put on the leather harness. I step into the shoes again, and walk.
    I will deliver

Letters, cards, important gifts. I roll up a sleeve, and put my
    hand into his pocket.
His wallet. I open up its creaking leather palms, and I am rich:
I see myself in this, his photograph of me. He coughs, and
    stirs; his hands
Begin to sleepwalk, as if managing Pinocchio's wooden limbs.

Wild rough seas tonight:
yawning over Sado Isle,
snowy galaxies.

            – Basho

Hamlet

As usual, the clock in The Clock Bar was a good few minutes
    fast:
A fiction no one really bothered to maintain, unlike the story
The comrade on my left was telling, which no one knew for
    certain truth:
Back in 1922, a sergeant, I forget his name, was shot outside the
    National Bank . . . .
Ah yes, what year was it that they knocked it down? Yet, its
    memory's as fresh
As the inky smell of new pound notes – which interferes with
    the beer-and-whiskey
Tang of now, like two dogs meeting in the revolutionary 69 of
    a long sniff,

Or cattle jostling shit-stained flanks in the Pound. For *pound, as some wag*
    some wag
Interrupted, was an off-shoot of the Falls, from the Irish, fál,
    a hedge;
Hence, *any kind of enclosed thing, its twigs and branches*
    commemorated
By the soldiers' drab and olive camouflage, as they try to melt
Into a brick wall; red coats might be better, after all. *At any rate,*
This sergeant's number came up; not a winning one. The bullet had his
    name on it.
Though Sergeant X, as we'll call him, doesn't really feature in the
    story:
The nub of it is, *This tin can which was heard that night, trundling down*
From the bank, down Balaklava Street. Which thousands heard,
    and no one ever
Saw. Which was heard for years, any night that trouble might be
Round the corner . . . and when it skittered to a halt, you knew
That someone else had snuffed it: a name drifting like an
    afterthought,
A scribbled wisp of smoke you try and grasp, as it becomes
    diminuendo, then
Vanishes: For *fál is also frontier, boundary, as in the undiscovered*
    country
From whose bourne no traveller returns, the illegible, thorny hedge of
    time itself –
Heartstopping moments, measured not by the pulse of a
    wristwatch, nor
The archaic anarchists' alarm clock, but a mercury tilt device
Which 'only connects' on any given bump on the road. So, by this
    wingèd messenger
The promise 'to pay the bearer' is fulfilled:

As someone buys another round, an Allied Irish Banks £10 note
    drowns in

The slops of the counter; a Guinness stain blooms on the artist's
    impression
Of the sinking of *The Girona*; a tiny foam hisses round the
    salamander brooch
Dredged up to show how love and money endure, beyond death
    and the Armada,
Like the bomb-disposal expert in his suit of salamander-cloth.
Shielded against the blast of time by a strangely mediaeval visor,
He's been outmoded by this jerky robot whose various
    attachments include
A large hook for turning over corpses that may be booby-trapped;
But I still have this picture of his hands held up to avert the future
In a final act of *No surrender*, as, twisting through the murky
    fathoms
Of what might have been, he is washed ashore as pearl and coral.

This *strange eruption to our state* is seen in other versions of the Falls:
A *no-go area, a ghetto, a demolition zone.* For the ghost, as it turns
    out –
All this according to your man, and I can well believe it – this tin
    ghost,
Since the streets it haunted were abolished, was never heard again.
The sleeve of Raglan Street has been unravelled; the helmet of
    Balaklava
Is torn away from the mouth. The dim glow of Garnet has gone
    out,
And with it, all but the memory of where I lived. I, too, heard the
    ghost:
A roulette trickle, or the hesitant annunciation of a downpour,
    ricocheting
Off the window; a goods train shunting distantly into a siding,
Then groaning to a halt; the rainy cries of children after dusk.
For the voice from the grave reverberates in others' mouths, as the
    sails

Of the whitethorn hedge swell up in a little breeze, and tremble
Like the spiral blossom of Andromeda: so suddenly are shrouds
    and branches
Hung with street-lights, celebrating all that's lost, as fields are
    reclaimed
By the Starry Plough. So we name the constellations, to put a
    shape
On what was there; so, the storyteller picks his way between the
    isolated stars.

But, *Was it really like that?* And, *Is the story true?*
You might as well tear off the iron mask, and find that no one,
    after all,
Is there: nothing but a cry, a summons, clanking out from the
    smoke
Of demolition. Like some son looking for his father, or the father
    for his son,
We try to piece together the exploded fragments. Let these broken
    spars
Stand for the Armada and its proud full sails, for even if
The clock is put to rights, everyone will still believe it's fast:
The barman's shouts of *time* will be ignored in any case, since
    time
Is conversation; it is the hedge that flits incessantly into the
    present,
As words blossom from the speakers' mouths, and the flotilla
    returns to harbour,
Long after hours.

from *First Language* (1994)

Second Language

English not being yet a language, I wrapped my lubber-lips
    around my thumb;
Brain-deaf as an embryo, I was snuggled in my comfort-blanket
    dumb.

Growling figures campaniled above me, and twanged their
    carillons of bronze
Sienna consonants embedded with the vowels *alexandrite, emerald*
    and *topaz.*

The topos of their discourse seemed to do with me and convoluted
    genealogy;
Wordy whorls and braids and skeins and spiral helices,
    unskeletoned from laminate geology –

How this one's slate-blue gaze is correspondent to another's new-
    born eyes;
Gentians, forget-me-nots, and cornflowers, diurnal in a heliotrope
    surmise.

Alexandrine tropes came gowling out like beagles, loped and
    unroped
On a snuffly Autumn. Nimrod followed after with his bold
    Arapahoes,

Who whooped and hollered in their unforked tongue. The trail
    was starred with
Myrrh and frankincense of Anno Domini; the Wise Men wisely
    paid their tariff.

A single star blazed at my window. Crepuscular, its acoustic
    perfume dims

And swells like flowers on the stanzaic-papered wall. Shipyard
    hymns

Then echoed from the East: gantry-clank and rivet-ranks, Six-
    County hexametric
Brackets, bulkheads, girders, beams, and stanchions; convocated
    and Titanic.

Leviathans of rope snarled out from ropeworks: disgorged
    hawsers, unkinkable lay,
Ratlines, S-twists, plaited halyards, Z-twists, catlines; all had
    their say.

Tobacco-scent and snuff breathed out in gouts of factory smoke
    like aromatic camomile;
Sheaves of brick-built mill-stacks glowered in the sulphur-
    mustard fog like campaniles.

The dim bronze noise of midnight-noon and Angelus then
    boomed and clinked in Latin
Conjugations; statues wore their shrouds of amaranth; the
    thurible chinked out its smoky patina.

I inhaled *amo, amas, amat* in quids of *pros* and *versus* and *Introibos*
Ad altare Del; incomprehensibly to others, spoke in Irish. I slept
    through the Introit.

The enormous Monastery surrounded me with nave and
    architrave. Its ornate pulpit
Spoke to me in fleurs-de-lys of Purgatory. Its sacerdotal gaze
    became my pupil.

My pupil's nose was bathed in Pharaonic unguents of dope and
    glue.

Flimsy tissue-paper plans of aeroplanes unfolded whimsical ideas
of the blue,

Where, unwound, the prop's elastic is unpropped and balsawood
extends its wings
Into the hazardous azure of April. It whirrs into the realm of
things.

Things are kinks that came in tubes; like glue or paint extruded,
that became
A hieroglyphic alphabet. Incestuous in pyramids, Egyptians were
becalmed.

I climbed into it, delved its passageways, its sepulchral interior,
its things of kings
Embalmed; sarcophagi, whose perfume I exhumed in chancy
versions of the I-Ching.

A chink of dawn was revelated by the window. Far-off cocks
crowed crowingly
And I woke up, verbed and tensed with speaking English; I lisped
the words so knowingly.

I love the as-yet morning, when no one's abroad, and I am like a
postman on his walk,
Distributing strange messages and bills, and arbitrations with
the world of talk:

I foot the snow and almost-dark. My shoes are crisp, and bite into
the blue-
White firmament of pavement. My father holds my hand and
goes blah-

Blah with me into the ceremonial dawn. I'm wearing tweed. The
    universe is Lent
And Easter is an unspun cerement, the gritty, knitty, tickly cloth
    of unspent

Time. I feel its warp and weft. Bobbins pirn and shuttle in
    Imperial
Typewriterspeak. I hit the keys. The ribbon-black chinks out the
    words in serial.

What comes next is next, and no one knows the *che sera* of it, but
    must allow
The Tipp-Ex present at the fingertips. Listen now: an angel
    whispers of the here-and-now.

The future looms into the mouth incessantly, gulped-at and
    unspoken;
Its guardian is intangible, but gives you hints and winks and
    nudges as its broken token.

I woke up blabbering and dumb with too much sleep. I rubbed
    my eyes and ears.
I closed my eyes again and flittingly, forgetfully, I glimpsed the
    noise of years.

Two to Tango

Whether you want to change your face or not's up to yourself. But
    the bunk of history
They'll make up for you. Someone else's shoes. They can put you
    anywhere. Where's a mystery.

Aromas, sounds, the texture of the roads, the heaviness or lightness
    of the air –
All these contribute to the sense of place. These things are what we
    are,

Though mitigated by ourselves. The details might be anywhere, so
    long as a romantic atmosphere
Is evoked. But to mention Africa, the Middle East or Russia is
    anathema.

It's not the money. Money enters into it, but doesn't talk. I do that.
I fill the blanks they know already. I'm the jammy centre in the
    doughnut.

Introspection must serve a purpose beyond the simple passing of
    time:
That bit of dialogue, recalled, might prove to be the clue that solves
    the crime.

And Belfast isn't like Beirut, although I've never been there. It's
    what it is:
Agendas, bricks and mortar, interfaces. Others in the structure like
    me. *Veritas.*

Dialogue can act as a transition bridge: for example, *I've been
    meaning to talk to you,*
He said, *I hear you've got the job . . . that you'll have to move to Tokyo . . .*

They can't let on I'm there. There's nothing down on paper. What
   there is is code.
Alone? I'm sometimes. Very. Very. Sometimes very hot and
   sometimes very cold.

She watched the way the hair on his wrist curled round the band of his
   wrist-watch:
This is an example of 'initial entanglement', from which it's
   difficult to wrench

Herself. Others might be fragrances, like melted candle-wax;
   sometimes, even, sweat.
And the timepiece might be Philippe Patek, but never, under any
   circumstances, *Swatch.*

You find ways around it, yawning, getting up to 'go out for a
   couple of hours.'
They make the place secure for you. It's like a Twilight Zone
   where they exert their Special Powers.

And you make sure you don't repeat yourself. Change the routine
   ever
So slightly. Tell no one, I mean no one, what you're up to. Never.
   Never. Never.

Use slang and buzz-words sparingly. Use body language tags,
   especially for men:
He punctuated his words with repeated clicks of his Mont Blanc ball-
   point pen.

For when you stop saying *never,* that's when you'll get dead.
   You'll put your sweet lips
A little too close to the phone and talk of *always* in a fatal
   momentary lapse.

And then you think, not to repeat yourself is not real life. And so
   you do.
You develop mannerisms. Tics and tags, without them looking
   like they're pseudo.

And contrast is important, between male and female dialogue.
   Then there's changes of identity;
But be careful of the cliché where the protagonist is torn between
   identical

Twins. A hero, me? I'm not. It's just a game. I'm saving lives?
   Perhaps.
It's like a sentence crammed with grammar, phrases, ages,
   hyphens, stops.

Is this a faction or a *roman fleuve* (more commonly called
   generational
Or *saga*)? Decide before you start, work out your plot, then go for
   it. Be *inspirational.*

One side says this, the other that. You work it out yourself and
   walk between the story lines.
What's true is what you do. Keep your head down. Know yourself.
   Ignore the starry skies.

Drunk Boat

After Rimbaud, Le Bateau Ivre

As I glided down the lazy Meuse, I felt my punters had gone
AWOL –
In fact, Arapahoes had captured them for target practice, nailing
them to stakes. Oh hell,

I didn't give a damn. I didn't want a crew, nor loads of Belgian
wheat, nor English cotton.
When the whoops and hollers died away, their jobs were well
forgotten.

Through the tug and zip of tides, more brain-deaf than an
embryo, I bobbled;
Peninsulas, unmoored and islanded, were envious of my Babel-
babble.

Storms presided at my maritime awakening. Like a cork I waltzed
across the waves,
Which some call sailors' graveyards; but I despised their far-off,
lighted enclaves.

As children think sour apples to be sweet, so the green sap
swamped the planks
And washed away the rotgut and the puke, the rudder and the
anchor-hanks.

I've been immersed, since then, in Sea Poetry, anthologized by
stars,
As through the greenish Milky Way a corpse drifts downwards,
clutching a corrupted spar;

When suddenly, those sapphire blues are purpled by Love's rusty
    red. No lyric
Alcohol, no Harp, can combat it, this slowly-pulsing, twilit
    panegyric.

I've known lightning, spouts, and undertows, maelstrom
    evenings that merge into Aurora's
Blossoming of doves. I've seen the Real Thing; others only get its
    aura.

I've seen the sun's demise, where seas unroll like violet, antique
Venetian blinds; dim spotlight, slatted by the backstage work of
    Ancient Greeks.

I dreamed the green, snow-dazzled night had risen up to kiss the
    seas'
Blue-yellow gaze, the million plankton eyes of phosphorescent
    argosies.

I followed then, for many months, the mad-cow waves of the
    Antipodes,
Oblivious to the Gospel of how Jesus calmed the waters, walking
    on his tippy-toes.

I bumped, you know, into the Floridas, incredible with pupil-
    flowers
And manatees, which panther-men had reined with rainbows
    and with Special Powers.

I saw a whole Leviathan rot slowly in the seething marsh, till it
    became
All grot and whalebone. Blind cataracts lurched into oubliettes,
    and were becalmed.

Glaciers and argent seas, pearly waves and firecoal skies! A
	tangled serpent-cordage
Hauled up from the Gulf, all black-perfumed and slabbered with
	a monster's verbiage!

I would have liked the children to have seen them: goldfish,
	singing-fish, John Dorys –
My unanchored ones, I'm cradled by the tidal flowers and lifted
	near to Paradise.

Sometimes, fed-up with the Poles and Zones, the sea would give a
	briny sob and ease
Off me; show me, then, her vented shadow-flowers, and I'd be
	like a woman on her knees . . . .

Peninsular, I juggled on my decks with mocking-birds and
	ostriches
And rambled on, until my frail lines caught another upside-
	down, a drowned Australian.

Now see me, snarled-up in the reefs of bladder-wrack, or thrown
	by the waterspout like craps
Into the birdless Æther, where Royal Navy men would slag my
	sea-drunk corpse –

Smoking, languorous in foggy violet, I breathed a fireglow patch
	into
The sky, whose azure trails of snot are snaffled by some Poets as
	an entrée –

Electromagnets, hoof-shaped and dynamic, drove the Nautilus.
	Black hippocampuses
Escorted it, while heat-waves drummed and blattered on the July
	campuses.

Me, I shivered: fifty leagues away, I heard the bumbling
	Behemoths and Scarabs;
Spider spinning in the emerald, I've drifted off the ancient
	parapets of Europe!

Sidereal archipelagoes I saw! Island skies, who madly welcomed
	the explorer;
O million starry birds, are these the endless nights you dream of
	for the Future?

I've whinged enough. Every dawn is desperate, every bitter sun.
	The moon's atrocious.
Let the keel split now, let me go down! For I am bloated, and the
	boat is stotious.

Had I some European water, it would be that cold, black puddle
Where a child once launched a paper boat – frail butterfly – into
	the dusk; and huddled

There, I am no more. O waves, you've bathed and cradled me and
	shaped
Me. I'll gaze no more at Blue Ensigns, nor merchantmen, nor the
	drawn blinds of prison-ships.

The Ballad of HMS Belfast

On the first of April, Belfast disengaged her moorings, and sailed
    away
From old Belfast. Sealed orders held our destination, somewhere
    in the Briny Say.

Our crew of Jacks was aromatic with tobacco-twist and alcoholic
Reekings from the night before. Both Catestants and Protholics,

We were tarry-breeked and pig-tailed, and sailed beneath the
    White Ensign;
We loved each other nautically, though most landlubbers
    thought we were insane.

We were full-rigged like the Beagle, piston-driven like the
    Enterprise
Express; each system was a back-up for the other, auxiliarizing
    verse with prose.

Our engines ticked and tacked us up the Lough, cranks and link-
    pins, cross-rods
Working ninety to the dozen; our shrouds and ratlines rattled
    like a cross-roads

Dance, while swivels, hook blocks, cleats, and fiddles jigged their
    semi-colons
On the staves. We staggered up the rigging like a bunch of demi-
    golems,

Tipsy still, and dreamed of underdecks – state-rooms, crystal
    chandeliers,
And saloon bars – until we got to gulp the ozone; then we swayed
    like gondoliers

Above the aqua. We gazed at imperceptible horizons, where amethyst
Dims into blue, and pondered them again that night, before the mast.

Some sang of Zanzibar and Montalban, and others of the lands unascertained
On maps; we entertained the Phoenix and the Unicorn, till we were grogged and concertina'ed.

We've been immersed, since then, in cruises to the Podes and Antipodes;
The dolphin and the flying fish would chaperone us like aquatic aunties

In their second, mermaid childhood, till we ourselves felt neither fish nor flesh, but
Breathed through gills of rum and brandy. We'd flounder on the randy decks like halibut.

Then our Captain would emerge to scold us from his three days' incommunicado
And promenaded on the poop-deck, sashed and epauletted like a grand Mikado

To bribe us with the Future: new Empires, Realms of Gold, and precious ore
Unheard-of since the days of Homer: we'd boldly go where none had gone before.

Ice to Archangel, tea to China, coals to Tyne: such would be our cargo.
We'd confound the speculators' markets and their exchequered, logical embargo.

Then were we like the Nautilus, that trawls the vast and purple
    catacomb
For cloudy shipwrecks, settled in their off-the-beam, intractable
    aplomb.

Electric denizens glide through the Pisan masts, flickering their
    Pisces' lumière;
We regard them with a Cyclops eye, from our bathyscope beneath
    la mer.

Scattered cutlery and dinner-services lie, hugger-mugger, on the
    murky floor.
An empty deck-chair yawns and undulates its awning like a
    semaphore.

Our rising bubble then went bloop, bloop till it burst the swaying
    window-pane;
Unfathomed from the cobalt deep, we breathed the broad Pacific
    once again.

Kon-Tiki-like, we'd drift for days, abandoning ourselves to all the
    elements,
Guided only by the aromatic coconut, till the wind brought us
    the scent of lemons –

Then we'd disembark at Vallambroso or Gibraltar to explore the
    bars;
Adorned in sequin-scales, we glimmered phosphorescently like
    stars

That crowd innumerably in midnight harbours. O olive-dark
    interior,
All splashed with salt and wine! Havana gloom within the
    humidor!

The atmosphere dripped heavy with the oil of anchovies, tobacco-
      smoke, and chaw;
We grew languorous with grass and opium and *kif*, the very best
      of draw,

And sprawled in urinous piazzas; slept until the fog-horn trump
      of Gabriel.
We woke, and rubbed our eyes, half-gargled still with
      braggadocio and garble.

And then the smell of docks and ropeworks. Horse-dung. The
      tolling of the Albert clock.
Its Pisan slant. The whirring of its ratchets. Then everything
      began to click:

I lay bound in iron chains, alone, my *aisling* gone, my sentence
      passed.
Grey Belfast dawn illuminated me, on board the prison ship
      Belfast.

from *Opera Et Cetera* (1994)

Eesti

I wandered homesick-lonely through that Saturday of silent Tallinn
When a carillon impinged a thousand raining quavers on my ear,
    tumbling

Dimly from immeasurable heights into imaginary brazen gong-space,
    trembling
Dimpled in their puddled, rain-drop halo-pools, concentrically
    assembling.

I glimpsed the far-off, weeping onion-domes. I was inveigled towards the
    church
Through an aural labyrinth of streets until I sheltered in its porch.

I thumbed the warm brass worn thumb-scoop of the latch. Tock. I entered
    into bronze-
Dark, shrines and niches lit by beeswax tapers and the sheen of ikons.

Their eyes and the holes in their hands were nailed into my gaze, quod
    erat demonstrandum:
Digits poised and pointed towards their hearts. They are beautiful
    Panjandrums

Invoked by murmuring and incense, hymns that father passes on to father,
The patina of faces under painted faces. They evoke another

Time, where I am going with you, father, to first Mass. We walked
The starry frozen pavement, holding hands to stop ourselves from falling.
    There was no talk,

Nor need for it. Our incense-breath was words enough as we approached
    the Gothic,
Shivering in top-coats, on the verge of sliding off the metronomic

Azure-gradual dawn, as nave and transept summoned us with beaded, thumbed

And fingered whispering. Silk-tasselled missals. Rosaries. Statues stricken dumb

Beneath their rustling purple shrouds, as candles wavered in the holy smoke.
The mosaic chapel echoed with a clinking, chinking censer-music.

This red-letter day would not be written, had I not wandered through the land of Eesti.
I asked my father how he thought it went. He said to me in Irish, Listen: Éist.

D

Whoever takes an arrow to this bow will really feel the slippery sap
Of the freshly-peeled sally-rod and the tensile spring of the future slap

Of the string, all imaginary targets riddled through with past plu-
Perfect hits and misses; the lucky shot of two birds skewered in the perfect blue.

All thumbs and fingers tweezerlike, I unbarbed his fletcher's herringbone,
Like I unstuck the hoops and loops of the Velcro Celtic Twilight Zone.

I unzipped it open, and so witnessed the opposing oars of quinquereme

And decked-out trireme, how they rowed majestically into
    Byzantium:

A shower of arrows welcomed them like needles to a magnet, like
    the whole
Assault of future into present, the way that the South attracts the
    North pole.

H

The Powers-that-Be decreed that from the — of — the sausage
    rolls, for reasons
Of security, would be contracted to a different firm. They gave
    the prisoners no reasons.

The prisoners complained. We cannot reproduce his actual words
    here, since their spokesman is alleged
To be a sub-commander of a movement deemed to be illegal.

An actor spoke for him in almost-perfect lip-synch: *It's not the
    quality*
We're giving off about. Just that it seems they're getting smaller. We're
    talking quantity.

His 'Belfast' accent wasn't West enough. Is the H in H-Block *aitch*
    or *haitch*?
Does it matter? *What we have we hold? Our day will come?* Give or
    take an inch?

Well, give an inch and someone takes an effing mile. Everything
    is in the ways
You say them. Like, the prison that we call Long Kesh is to the
    Powers-that-Be *The Maze.*

K

K is the leader of the empty orchestra or karaoke.
K is the conductor on the wrong bus that you took today and
    landed you in yesterday.

Where everything was skew. The rainbow colours were all out of
    kilter,
Like oil had leaked out all over the road from a dropped and
    broken philtre.

There, no one wanted to be recognised, and walked around in
    wrap-round
Polaroids. There was Semtex in the Maxwell House, and twenty
    shillings in the pound.

K came into it again, with the sidelong, armed stance of a
    Pharaoh.
He took my kopeck, docked it with two holes, and told me it was
    time to go.

All the motor-cars were black. I got behind the wheel of one. It
    worked O.K.
Welder's sparks zipped from the trolley. The radio was playing
    karaoke.

L

I'm always sitting in the wrong corner of the room or in the
    wrong angle,
So that part of it is hidden from me always. Like you are in the
    ingle-

Nook and I am not, or you are upstairs ironing. I can nearly hear
    the hiss
As the *Sunbeam* hits the aromatic damp of cloth. It's like a breathy
    kiss,

The warm snog of a freshly-pressed cotton shirt I put on for the
    interview.
Like, I don't know who's upright, who is horizontal. But the L is
    me and you.

As the ironing board remembers it, it bears a burnt Sienna scorch
Of memory. For all its *this* and *that* and *is* and *was* it carries a
    torch.

I felt like the girl in a hairdresser's, flicking backwards through
    an issue of *Elle,*
As it gets dark outside. A momentary train passed by with lighted
    windows on the El.

M

When M is amplified among the gongs and incense, it becomes
    an *om*
Resounding in the saffron gloom. Smoke rises up as if from
    meerschaum.

It's a sort of unusual Vermeer, with pewter mugs and dogs drunk
    under
The table. Hanging from the ceiling is a caged *macaco* monkey,
    ponder-

Ing the digits of her basic American Sign Language for *nuts*. They
    bring
Her beer instead. Outside, on the icy mere, the families are
    skating.

It is beautiful to breathe the civic, clean, cold-stone-sober air after
    all that smoke,
To see the skated babies slithering around in Babygros under
    older folk,

While in the artist's back yard, drawers and bras and shirts and
    pinafores are fro-
Zen on a line; stiffened overnight, they're creaking to and fro.

O

The tea-cup stain on the white damask table-cloth was not quite
    perfect. Never-
Theless, I'd set my cup exactly on it, like it was a stain-remover.

I sipped the rim with palatable lip. I drank the steaming liquor
    up.
My granny then would read my future from the tea-leaves'
    leavings in the cup.

I stared into enormous china O and saw its every centrifugal flaw,
The tiny bobbles glazed in its interior of Delphic oracle. I yawned

Into its incandescent blaze of vowel like the cool of dudes in black
    fedoras
At high noon; trigger-fingered, shadowless, they walked beneath
    sombreros.

They stopped me inadvertently and asked for my identity. I did
    not know
Until the mouth of a gun was pressed against my forehead, and I
    felts its O.

S

The train slowed to a halt with a sigh like *Schweppes*. I see you
    now, Miranda,
Through the glassed-in cloudy steam of yesteryear. Do you
    remember, Miranda,

The archaic of when I met you first, that time when all the
    motor-cars were black?
My heartache? I did not stand out from the crowd, I was a stand-
    in in a claque.

And you were Carmen, Miranda, you were Madama Butterfly.
    You were prox-
Opera, the roles that you insinuated into. And you knew you
    were it. Those parox-

Ysms of grief! Those swooning cadences! Those rolling eyes and
    Rs! The spotlight
Kissed you as the claque went crazy, hurling flowers and lire at
    you. It was out of sight.

And I was there, Miranda, in the empty theatre, picking up your
    petals. I walked on plush.
I felt I was the silent *s* in *aisle*. And where were you, Miranda?
    Hush.

U

The urchin is a hedgehog, hence its corallaceous spines. It's made
    its U
Into a balled-up Erinacean O of Rimbaud green or blue,
    depending how you

See it. It is a self-protective device, like the independent eye
Of the chameleon, or the stripes on a zebra crossing. It's the
    amber eye

Of the traffic lights. It's a corona – not Havana, but the sound-
    horn
Of a daffodil, emitting blue stars from its halo crown of thorns.

If you drive over one, it gets squashed, so you often come across
Them flattened, parchment-like on rural roads, especially in
    poems like this.

Their *Zeitgeist* is reverse, if *verse* means *the turn at the end of a furrow.*
They propagate themselves by not eating their own farrow.

Y

It's only now that I recall the catapult I cut from the ash tree,
How I bound with wire to the tangs of its fork an elastic strip
    snipped out free-

Hand from a long-deflated inner tube. Not to forget the leather
    thing-
Amajig for holding the stone or whatever. I guess you call it the
    sling.

But the sling is, I think, the elastic too. There must be a language
    of slang,
Some children's twang where words hit home, dit-dah, to the
    Auld Lang

Syne of what they were, and why. As if the marble shot had
    boomeranged
And got you right between the teeth, just to remind you it was
    no meringue.

Still, I try to bite into it. Then I did. Nothing happened. I thought
    on,
A thong of stretched elastic swish. Then I hit the recall button.

Z

The ultimate buzz is the sound of sleep or of bees, or the slalom
    I'll
Make through the dark pines of a little-known Alp on my
    snowmobile.

You will hear me fading and droning towards you from the valley
    next
To one, for I have miles to go: when I deliver all the letters, that's
    the text.

The canvas sack on my back reminds me I am in the archaic
    footprints
Of my postman father. I criss and cross the zig-zag precedents.

Snow is falling fast, my parallels already blurring on the
    mountainside,
But I am flying towards you through the stars on skis of
    Astroglide.

In the morning you will open up the envelope. You will get
    whatever
Message is inside. It is for all time. Its postmark is 'The Twelfth of
    Never'.

Graecum Est: Non Legitur

The fly made an audible syzygy as it dive-bombed through the
    dormer
And made a rendezvous with this, the page I'm writing on. It was
    its karma.

This tsetse was a Greek to me, making wishy-washy gestures
    with its hands
And feet. I made to brush it off, before it vaulted off into a
    handstand

Ceiling-corner of the room. It dithered over to the chandelier-flex
And buzzed around it upside down in a stunt-plane Camel helix.

The landing-page approached my craft as I began to think again.
    The candle guttered.
My enormous hand was writing on the wall. The words began to
    stutter

As the quill ran out. *Syzygy:* His dizzy Nibs was back. I took on
    board more ink.
He staggered horse-like towards the blue blot I'd just dropped.
    Then he began to drink.

Cave Quid Dicis, Quando, et Cui

You will recognise them by their Polaroids that make the span
    between their eyes
Immeasurable. Beware their digital watches; they are bugged
    with microscopic batteries.

Make sure you know your left from right and which side of the
    road you walk on.
If one stops beside you and invites you in, do not enter the
    pantechnicon.

You'd be participating in another's house removal. You could
    become
A part of the furniture, slumped in some old armchair. That
    would be unwelcome.

Welcome is the mat that does not spell itself. Words don't speak
    as loud as deeds,
Especially when the safety is off. Watch it if they write in screeds,

For everything you say is never lost, but hangs on in the starry
    void
In ghosted thumb-whorl spiral galaxies. Your fingerprints are
    everywhere. *Be paranoid.*

Labuntur et Imputantur

It was overcast. No hour at all was indicated by the gnomon.
With difficulty I made out the slogan, *Time and tide wait for no
man.*

I had been waiting for you, Daphne, underneath the dripping
laurels, near
The sundial glade where first we met. I felt like Hamlet on the
parapets of Elsinore,

Alerted to the ectoplasmic moment, when Luna rends her
shroud of cloud
And sails into a starry archipelago. Then your revenant appeared
and spake aloud:

*I am not who you think I am. For what we used to be is gone. The
moment's over,
Whatever years you thought we spent together. You don't know the story.
And moreover,*

You mistook the drinking-fountain for a sundial. I put my lips to its
whatever,
And with difficulty I made out the slogan, *Drink from me and you
shall live forever.*

Quod Erat Demonstrandum

She was putting together her Cinderella outfit in the usual
    sequin
Sequence she'd bought as pocket galaxies. The headless armless
    mannequin

Was on her mind from yesterday's shop window, as she
    approached her
Doppelgänger in the glass. Suddenly no sisters, as the pumpkin
    coached her

To the ball, drawn by the equine mice. The palace floor was disco-
    glitter stars
She polished, gliding in her fur-soled slippers. The Prince, just
    back from the wars –

Whatever wars they were – escorted her, unscarred by his
    experience.
'He'll make an extremely good king, whatever "being a good
    king" means',

The door-mouse whispered to me through his epaulette. 'Things
    will evolve. You see,
I knew him as a frog, and she's no tailor's dummy. Q.E.D.'

The Poet as Snow-Merchant

When spring has sprung and disappeared the snow, and
    youngsters want to laugh at grown-
Ups, but find – instead of snowdrifts – brothers, parents (ready-
    made folk), then the clown

Appears, this crazy who sells snow. Hibernian winter permafrosts
    his soul;
He haggles like a lunatic with naked trees, his frozen birds and
    ice-floes

Creaking like somnivolent Antarctica. He speaks of seeds as
    unexploded
Atom bombs. Swans drift by in caravanserai across the colour-
    coded

Blue ice of one eye; you could catch a pike in the pupil-black
    bullet-hole
Drilled in the other. He hawks his merchandise remorselessly,
    and being snow

Himself, he spreads himself about: a scattered aftermath of
    downy pillow-
Feathers marks the progress of his unseen army, in which all the
    jolly fellows
Carry brooms instead of ostrich plumes; the mayor's statue they
    denounce as being hollow.

A Pair

All human kind deserves love. But the lunatic who tries to plait a
rope
Of sand in order to lasso the newly-risen moon, and by this trope

Be levitated; the other dope who, stooped over a river of gold,
spends all
His life in moulding it to the shape of the faceless wind, to give
us all

A newly-minted coinage: this odd pair can hitch themselves to
my star
Any time. And when I'm not at home, you'll know for sure they
are.

Delta

The blues they make down there come out of Mason jars and
sinsemilla cigarettes,
The hollers of the whippoorwill, the clicking of cicadas' castanets.

They have sold their souls to many devils. They're the alcohol in
syllabub.
They phrase their wired-up twelve-bar syllables with accents of
Beelzebub.

Broken bottle-necks are popular for stabbing, or for sliding on
steel strings.
A knife would do as well, as, hunched over his azure guitar, the
blind man sings

Of doom and gloom, of snakes in rooms, the various uses of a
   coffee-spoon,
Of sugar, tea, and locks, and keys, how everything goes mostly to
   this tune:

Woke up this morning, blues were on my mind. I put the record on. It
   wouldn't go.
I pulled up the blind. The sunlight was too loud. I put on shades
   of indigo.

Oscar

I held the figurine aloft, revelling in my actor's gravestone smile;
I boldly faced an orchestra of flash, as paparazzi packed the aisle.

I thanked everyone: all those who'd made it possible for me to be,
Down to the midwife and my grade-school teacher; my analyst;
   the Committee;

Not forgetting William Shakespeare, who had writ the script on
   vellum,
Nor the born anachronist director, who had set it in the *ante*
   bellum –

The way he saw it, Hamlet was a kind of Southern dude who
   chewed cheroots.
He wanted Vivien to play Ophelia Leigh. The uncle was a *putz.*

So, everybody, give a big hand to *All Our Yesterdays,* this apron
   weft
And warp of life we strut upon a brief while, till *All exeunt, stage*
   left.

Tango

It's all long steps and pauses, where the woman uses the man as a
   crutch;
Ironically, it is unlikely that it comes from the Latin verb 'to
   touch'.

It is not the foxtrot nor the frug, still less the polka-dot or
   rigadoon;
Zapateado, tarantella, rhumba, mambo, allemande, it's not. It is a
   swoon

Of music, castanetted by the clicking silver buttons of the square
   bandoneon,
Which is its instrument, bass-and-treble toned like the
   chameleon:

Beautiful gloomy levity of camouflage, like when the girl's bolero
Creaks against the moustachioed starched shirt, as he struts and
   pansies in torero

Mode. He leans into her quickstep jitterbug. Her legs are all
   akimbo
As he shimmies lower, lower, entering the possibility of limbo.

Zulu

At last, I remember the half-broomstick assegai with which I
    used to kill
Imaginary soldiers. I danced around them like a hound of
    Baskerville.

I faced the typecast phalanxes of English, shielded only by a
    dustbin-
Lid; sometimes, I'd *sotto voce* whistle 'The Dragoons of Inniskillin',

Till an Agincourt of arrows overwhelm'd me, shot by Milton,
    Keats and Shakespeare,
And I became a redskin, foraging behind the alphabetic frontier.

Pale boldface wagons drew themselves into a hurried O of
    barricade;
Mounted on my hobby-horse, I whooped so much, I had to take a
    slug of orangeade.

I loved its cold-jolt glug and fizz, tilted bottle upheld like a
    trumpet
To the sun; or so it might be, in the gargled doggerel of this
    dumb poet.

from *The Alexandrine Plan* (1998)

Le Dormeur du val

C'est un trou de verdure où chante une rivière
Accrochant follement aux herbes des haillons
D'argent: où le soleil, de la montagne fière,
Luit: c'est un petit val qui mousse de rayons.

Un soldat jeune, bouche ouverte, tête nue,
Et la nuque baignant dans le frais cressons bleu,
Dort; il est étendu dans l'herbe, sous la nue,
Pâle dans son lit vert où la lumière pleut.

Les pieds dans les glaïeuls, il dort. Souriant comme
Sourirait un enfant malade, il fait un somme:
Nature, berce-le chaudement: il a froid.

Les parfums ne font pas frissonner sa narine;
Il dort dans le soleil, la main sur sa poitrine
Tranquille. Il a deux trous rouges au côté droit.

The Sleeper in the Valley

It's a greeny dip where a crazy guggling rill
Makes silver tatters of itself among the grass;
Where the sun pours down from the wild high mountain-sill;
It foams with light like bubbles in a champagne glass.

A soldier sleeps there, tousle-headed, mouth agape,
The nape of his neck drenched in cool blue watercress;
He's sprawled on the grass beneath a seething cloudscape,
Pale in the dew which oozes like juice from a wine-press.

His boots among the lilies, he lies sleeping, smiling
The smile of a sick child, cradle-head reclining.
Nature, rock him in your bosom warmly: he is cold.

No mortal smell assails his nostrils now; he's fast
Asleep, left hand on his heart. He's found peace at last.
Come closer: there, in his right side, are two red holes.

Ma Bohème

(Fantaisie)

Je m'en allais, les poings dans mes poches crevées;
Mon paletot aussi devenait idéal;
J'allais sous le ciel, Muse! et j'étais ton féal;
Oh! là là! que d'amours splendides j'ai rêvées!

Mon unique culotte avait un large trou.
– Petit Poucet rêveur, j'égrenais dans ma course
Des rimes. Mon auberge était à la Grande-Ourse.
– Mes étoiles au ciel avaient un doux frou-frou.

Et je les écoutais, assis au bord des routes,
Ces bons soirs de septembre où je sentais des gouttes
De rosée à mon front, comme un vin de vigueur;

Où, rimant au milieu des ombres fantastiques,
Commes des lyres, je tirais les élastiques
De mes souliers blessés, un pied près de mon cœur!

On the Road

Thumbs hitched into my holey pockets, off I hiked
In my has-been-through-the-wars ex-Army greatcoat;
Under your blue skies, O muse, you took me on your bike;
I loved the way in which we spun in perfect rote.

My trousers had a hole as big as any arse,
And I became a dwarf who scatters rhymes along
The Milky Way. In the Great Bear, I sang my song,
As huge stars shivered in the rustling universe.

And I listened to their dew of blue September
Evenings fall on me, like Long Ago remembered
In the first sip of a cool green bubble-beaded wine;

I strummed the black elastic of my tattered boot
Held to my heart like youthful violin or lute,
A veritable pop-star of the awful rhyme.

Bohémiens en voyage

La tribu prophétique aux prunelles ardentes
Hier s'est mise en route, emportant ses petits
Sur son dos, ou livrant à leurs fiers appétits
Le trésor toujours prêt des mamelles pendantes.

Les hommes vont à pied sous leurs armes luisantes
Le long des chariots où les leurs son blottis,
Promenant sur le ciel des yeux appesantis
Par le morne regret des chimères absentes.

Du fond de son réduit sablonneux, le grillon,
Les regardant passer, redouble sa chanson;
Cybèle, qui les aime, augmente ses verdures,

Fait couler le rocher et fleurir le désert
Devant ces voyageurs, pour lesquels est ouvert
L'empire familier des ténèbres futures.

Travellers

Yesterday they hit the road again, that augury
Of prognosticators, babies papoosed to their backs,
Or dangling from their paps as big as haversacks,
Snuggled in a thoughtful, sucking reverie.

Shotguns held aloft, these far-flung sons of Araby
Accompany the wagons like Jack Kerouacs
Who view the stars as campfires for their bivouacs
Of yesteryear, and all its future lullaby.

From the cool depth of his sandy nook, the cricket,
Watching their procession, punches out a ticket
Of redoubled song, innumerable green shoots

Of waterfalling noise that makes the desert flower
At these nomad stops or steps of arbitrary hour,
When what's to be and what has been are in cahoots.

Le Couvercle

En quelque lieu qu'il aille, ou sur mer ou sur terre,
Sous un climat de flamme ou sous un soleil blanc,
Serviteur de Jésus, courtisan de Cythère,
Mendiant ténébreux ou Crésus rutilant,

Citadin, campagnard, vagabond, sédentaire,
Que son petit cerveau soit actif ou soit lent,
Partout l'homme subit la terreur du mystère,
Et ne regarde en haut qu'avec un œil tremblant.

En haut, le Ciel! ce mur de caveau qui l'étouffe,
Plafond illuminé pour un opéra bouffe
Où chaque histrion foule un sol ensanglanté;

Terreur du libertin, espoir du fol ermite;
Le Ciel! couvercle noir de la grande marmite
Où bout l'imperceptible et vaste Humanité.

The Lid

Take anyone who goes on land, or sea, or foam,
In torrid zones, or under snowblind Arctic suns,
Courtesans of Jesus, queuers at the stately home
Of Cythera, the gloomy beggars, and the big guns,

Staid citizens, and countrymen, and rolling stones,
All those whose brains are quick or slow, the bastard sons
Of all of us, who sprawl our incognizant bones
Beneath the Universe, like Godforsaken nuns:

Above us is the sky, this roof of sepulchre,
This comic opera ceiling lit by smoky sulphur,
Where the actors slither on a blood-drenched stage,

Terror of free-thinkers, hope of crazy hermits,
Black sky, pot-lid under which we seethe like termites,
And the recipe's last words say, Boil for an age.

Le Mort joyeux

Dans une terre grasse et pleine d'escargots
Je veux creuser moi-même une fosse profonde,
Où je puisse à loisir étaler mes vieux os
Et dormir dans l'oubli comme un requin dans l'onde.

Je hais les testaments et je hais les tombeaux;
Plutôt que d'implorer une larme du monde,
Vivant, j'aimerais mieux inviter les corbeaux
À saigner tour les bouts de ma carcasse immonde.

Ô vers! noirs compagnons sans oreille et sans yeux,
Voyez venir à vous un mort fibre et joyeux;
Philosopher viveurs, fils de la pourriture,

À travers ma ruine allez donc sans remords,
Et dites-moi s'il est encor quelque torture
Pour ce vieux corps sans âme et mort parmi les morts!

O Happy Death

In this muck, thick with crawling slugs, I'll dig a Deep
For me, in which my bones can stretch out in the dark,
At ease within a long oblivion of sleep,
Residing like an underwater dormant shark.

I hate testaments and graves. Such expensive upkeep
I can do without. I'd much prefer, while yet a spark
Remains in me, to let my suppurating heap
Be living meat for crows who utter cries of *quark*!

Accept, O worms – my *noir* compatriots, *sans* eyes, *sans* ears –
This dead free happy body of a sonneteer
As menu for your gourmet metamorphic tract;

Delve and seethe and eel into my ruined corpus;
Tell me all the tortures I must re-enact.
Then consult me under 'death' in your thesaurus.

'Le vierge, le vivace et le bel aujourd'hui…'

Le vierge, le vivace et le bel aujourd'hui
Va-t-il nous déchirer avec un coup d'aile ivre
Ce lac dur oublié que hante sous le givre
Le transparent glacier des vols qui n'ont pas fui!

Un cygne d'autrefois se souvient que c'est lui
Magnifique mais qui sans espoir se délivre
Pour n'avoir pas chanté la région où vivre
Quand du stérile hiver a resplendi l'ennui.

Tout son col secouera cette blanche agonie
Par l'espace infligée à l'oiseau qui le nie,
Mais non l'horreur du sol où le plumage est pris.

Fantôme qu'à ce lieu son pur éclat assigne,
Il s'immobilise au songe froid de mépris
Que vêt parmi l'exil inutile le Cygne.

At the Sign of the Swan

The beautiful today, untouched by human hand,
Swings towards us with a stagger of its drunken wing
To crash the frozen lake as cold as anything,
Ghosted by the glacial distances it never spanned!

A fabled swan the image of an ampersand
Is mute, for all his freed necessity to sing
His icy habitat of winter's fosterling,
Where dim suns yawned their tedium across the land.

His whole neck shudders off this agony of white
Impressed upon him by the spacey ambient light,
But not the Earth, where he's incapable of flight.

Beautiful ghost, condemned by his own brilliant line,
Engraved within a pond of icy crystallite,
He maintains the useless exile of a Swan, or sign.

Le Sonneur

Cependant que la cloche éveille sa voix claire
À l'air pur et limpide et profund du matin
Et passe sur l'enfant qui jette pour lui plaire
Un angélus parmi la lavande et le thym,

Le sonneur effleuré par l'oiseau qu'il éclaire,
Chevauchant tristement en geignant du latin
Sur la pierre qui tend la corde séculaire,
N'entend descendre à lui qu'un tintement lointain.

Je suis cet homme. Hélas! de la nuit désireuse,
J'ai beau tirer le câble sonner l'Idéal,
De froids péchés s'ébat un plumage féal,

Et la voix ne me vient que par bribes et creuse!
Mais, un jour, fatigué d'avoir en vain tiré,
Ô Satan, j'ôterai la pierre et me pendrai.

The Sonneteer

While the bell dings its bright pebbles of limpid sound
Into the stream of morning air, and skims the limbs
Of a small child who, wanting to chime in, propounds
An Angelus of lavender and thyme-blue hymns,

The lonely campanologist, within his bound
Of stony Latin, hears its bird-call interims
As muted, brittle tinkles on his turnaround
Of ancient rope he's trying to haul into him.

I am that man. Alas! Most nights I dangle on
An anxious tangled cable, while my entourage
Of sins flits round me in their gaudy camouflage,

And the bell croaks the last words of a wasted Don!
But one of these fine days, abandoning all hope,
I'll hang myself, O Satan, with the self-same rope.

La Géante

Du temps que la Nature en sa verve puissante
Concevait chaque jour des enfants monstrueux,
J'eusse aimé vivre auprès d'une jeune géante,
Comme aux pieds d'une reine un chat voluptueux.

J'eusse aimé voir son corps fleurir avec son âme
Et grandir librement dans ses terribles jeux;
Deviner si son cœur couve une sombre flamme
Aux humides brouillards qui nagent dans ses yeux;

Parcourir à loisir ses magnifiques formes;
Ramper sur le versant de ses genoux énormes,
Et parfois en été, quand les soleils malsains,

Lasse, la font s'étendre à travers la campagne,
Dormir nonchalamment à l'ombre de ses seins,
Comme un hameau paisible au pied d'une montagne.

The Maid of Brobdingnag

Long ago, when Nature, zanily extravagant,
Engendered monster bouncing babies every day,
I would have been inclined to live beside a giant
Girl, to be the loyal cat that sniffs her negligée.

I would have loved to watch her body flourishing
In tandem with her soul, developing her play
Of Juno games, to ponder on her nourishing
Some flame within her eyes of dark communiqué.

I would love to be a leisurely explorer
Of her Mount Parnassus, all the foothills of her,
When she sprawls herself on heat-dazed summer meadows;

And I could chill out in the shadow of her lapsed
Titanic body in these regions where I doze,
A hamlet overlooked by snowy Alpine paps.

La Vie antérieure

J'ai longtemps habité sous de vastes portiques
Que les soleils marins teignaient de mille feux,
Et que leurs grands piliers, droits et majestueux,
Rendaient pareils, le soir, aux grottes basaltiques.

Les houles, en roulant les images des cieux,
Mêlaient d'une façon solennelle et mystique
Les tout-puissants accords de leur riche musique
Aux couleurs du couchant reflété par mes yeux.

C'est là que j'ai vécu dans les voluptés calmes,
Au milieu de l'azur, des vagues, des splendeurs
Et des esclaves nus, tout imprégnés d'odeurs,

Qui me refraîchissaient le front avec des palmes,
Et dont l'unique soin était d'approfondir
Le secret douloureux qui me faisait languir.

I Had a Life

I lived for centuries beneath vast porticos
Illuminated by a thousand oceanic
Suns; at evening, steep columns of volcanic
Rock maintained a Fingal's Cave of glowering repose.

Tidal surges dimmed and swelled their dialectic
Of the skies above in powerful chords of rose
And hyacinth, while cascades of organic music
Interwove their harmonies of mellow yellows.

I dwelt there for an age of calm voluptuousness
In azure splendour, waited-on by naked slaves,
Whose perfumes wafted over me in brackish waves,

Whose cool palms soothed my burning forehead, saying, 'Yes,
Our only care is to appreciate your fear,
The poet's secret grief which makes you languish here.'

La Cloche fêlée

Il est amer et doux, pendant les nuits d'hiver,
D'écouter, près du feu qui palpite et qui fume,
Les souvenirs lointains lentement s'élever
Au bruit des carillons qui chantent dans la brume.

Bienheureuse la cloche aù gosier vigoureux
Qui, malgré sa vieillesse, alerte et bien portante,
Jette fidèlement son cri religieux,
Ainsi qu'un vieux soldat qui veille sous la tente!

Moi, mon âme est fêlée, et lorsqu'en ses ennuis
Elle veut de ses chants peupler l'air froid des nuits,
Il arrive souvent que sa voix affaiblie

Semble le râle épais d'un blessé qu'on oublie
Au bord d'un lac de sang, sous un grand tas de morts,
Et qui meurt, sans bouger, dans d'immenses efforts.

The Dongless Bell

On these long winter nights, it's bitter-sweet to sit
Beside the fire, and listen to it buzz and rhyme
With slowly-palpitating memories, which flit
Among the gongy noise of fog-bound midnight chimes.

Happy is the bell with a big, bronze sounding-bow,
Which, through the centuries, maintains its full aplomb
Of voice to broadcast to the faithful down below,
A veteran on watch before a regal tomb!

But as for me, I'm all shook up, my soul is flawed
With stress I can't articulate; I feel a fraud.
The wonky pitch of me sounds out an SOS,

Choked in the throat like the last gasp of a legless
God-abandoned conscript trapped beneath a heap of dead,
Who tries to speak, and leaves his final words unsaid.

La Beauté

Je suis belle, ô mortels! comme un rêve de pierre,
Et mon sein, où chacun s'est meurtri tour à tour,
Est fait pour inspirer au poète un amour
Éternel et muet ainsi que la matière.

Je trône dans l'azur comme un sphinx incompris;
J'unis un cœur de neige à la blancheur des cygnes;
Je hais le mouvement qui déplace les lignes,
Et jamais je ne pleure et jamais je ne ris.

Les poètes, devant mes grandes attitudes,
Que j'ai l'air d'emprunter aux plus fiers monuments,
Consumeront leurs jours en d'austères études;

Car j'ai, pour fasciner ces dociles amants,
De purs miroirs qui font toutes choses plus belles:
Mes yeux, mes larges yeux aux clartés éternelles!

Beauty

I am beautiful, O mortals, as a marble dream
Designed to terrify you with the silence
Of the stars, and everything within their ambience.
And you have bruised yourselves on me; such is your theme.

I am couched in the blue like an unblinking Sphinx
Who unifies a snowy heart with whiteness of the swan.
And nothing will disturb my alexandrine plan;
I do not weep, nor smile. So everybody thinks.

Poets sprawl before my monumental attitude
Like men inspired by statues of the former wars,
Who spend their nights in studying beatitude;

For, to fascinate them, I have giant mirrors
Which illuminate and magnify everything.
So stare into my vast eternal eyes, and sing.

from *The Twelfth of Never* (1998)

St Tib's Eve: Never. A corruption of St Ubes. There is no such
saint in the calendar as St Ubes, and therefore her eve falls on
the 'Greek Kalends'; neither before Christmas Day nor after it.
– Brewer's Dictionary of Phrase and Fable

Tib's Eve

There is a green hill far away, without a city wall,
Where cows have longer horns than any that we know;
Where daylight hours behold a moon of indigo,
And fairy cobblers operate without an awl.

There, ghostly galleons plough the shady Woods of True,
And schools of fishes fly among the spars and shrouds;
Rivers run uphill to spill into the starry clouds,
And beds of strawberries grow in the ocean blue.

This is the land of the green rose and the lion lily,
Ruled by Zeno's eternal tortoises and hares,
Where everything is metaphor and simile:

Somnambulists, we stumble through this paradise
From time to time, like words repeated in our prayers,
Or storytellers who convince themselves that truths are lies.

The Poppy Battle

She wore the bit of the poppy between her teeth
Like a wound or a salve, while the ritual salt
Was spilled. The Civic Guards performed a somersault,
Then cleared their throats in salvo as she laid the wreath.

The former puppet languished in an unmarked grave.
I'd read about it in a powder magazine.
Light glittered on a detail of the architrave
In military hospitals that reeked of gangrene.

Red crepe fake felt paper poppy petals with their dot
Of laudanum in everybody's buttonhole
Exuded empty perfumes of Forget-me-not.

I dreamed they had inhabited the planet Mars
With shell-shocked, pockmarked soldiers on a long parole:
Poppy the emblem of Peace and the Opium Wars.

Salt of the Earth

'Nodding buds with four crumpled petals, showy red,
Orange or white flowers, exuding milky juice' –
Was this the Soldier, Red-rag, Cusk, or Poppy-head?
The Sleepy-pap, or Fire-flout, Ceasefire or Truce?

STC gazed at the page illuminated
By a candle as he sprinkled his thesaurus
Over it to see the words hallucinated
Into sentences. He felt like Saul at Tarsus.

Whole fields in Flanders and Kent are salted with them.
Good farmers do not like to see them in the corn,
And call them cankers, whose growth they find difficult to stem.

Children's eyes are dazzled by these Thunder-flowers;
Crumpled Coleridge took an age to be re-born –
Poppy the emblem of Death and the Special Powers.

Nine Hostages

I cut my hand off at the wrist and threw it at the shore.
The goblin spilled a bag of red gold in my lap.
He wore emerald boots and a bloody fine cap.
Let Erin remember the days of yore.

I'd been riding the piebald mushroom for some time,
Following the Admiral's vermilion cruise.
He wore a blue cocked hat and tattered tartan trews.
We were both implicated in the crime of rhyme.

Up in the deep blue like a red balloon I flew,
Following the sickle grin of Old Man Moon.
Gun-metal gunships sailed in through the foggy dew.

In Creggan churchyard last night I fell into a dream
Confronted by a red dragoon, a green gossoon.
The red hand played the harp with oars of quinquereme.

The Rising of the Moon

As down by the glenside I met an old colleen,
She stung me with the gaze of her nettle-green eyes.
She urged me to go out and revolutionize
Hibernia, and not to fear the guillotine.

She spread the madder red skirts of her liberty
About my head so I was disembodied.
I fell among the People of No Property,
Who gave me bread and salt, and pipes of fragrant weed.

The pale moon was rising above the green mountain,
The red sun declining beneath the blue sea,
When I saw her again by yon clear crystal fountain,

Where poppies, not potatoes, grew in contraband.
She said, *You might have loved me for eternity.*
I kissed her grass-green lips, and shook her bloodless hand.

The Rising Sun

As I was driven into smoky Tokyo,
The yen declined again. It had been going down
All day against the buoyant Hibernian Pound.
Black rain descended like a harp arpeggio.

The Professor took me to a bonsai garden
To imbibe some thimblefuls of Japanese poteen.
We wandered through the forest of the books of Arden.
The number of their syllables was seventeen.

122

I met a maiden of Hiroshima who played
The hammer dulcimer like psychedelic rain.
The rising sun was hid behind a cloud of jade.

She sang to me of Fujiyama and of Zen,
Of yin and yang, and politics, and crack cocaine,
And Plato's caverns, which are measureless to men.

Dark Rosaleen

The songlines were proceeding at a daily pace
Like invisible barbed wire or whitethorn fences,
Running through the Monday of the market-place,
Where fellows mongered ballads under false pretences.

The port was packed with mountebanks and picketpocks,
Highwaymen on holiday, and soldiers on the spree.
Female sailors festered in the feisty docks,
And ragged rascals played the Game without a Referee.

I caught one by his buttonhole, and asked him plain
And proud, if ever dear old Ireland would be free,
Or would our forces be forever split in twain?

Could we expect the promised help from Papal Spain?
He caught my eye, and answered me quite candidly,
The only freedom that you'll find is in the dead domain.

The Tailor's Twist

It was clear the cluricaune had taken my bitch
Again last night for a ride, from her tattered pelt
And her poor ribs ranged in patches like a bacon flitch.
He did not reckon on the cunning of the Celt.

I stitched her back together with a spider's thread
And, with my foxglove thimble, gave her magic powers.
Next night, I laid out dribs of poteen, salt, and bread.
The cluricaune came for them in the early hours.

I watched him feed his face with food and salt and drink
Till, satisfied, he tried to jump my canine chum.
She twitched, and held him fast, and he began to shrink.

Then I put on my jacket of the hunting pink.
I penned his neck between my finger and my thumb,
And stuck the bastard's neb into a well of ink.

Catmint Tea

The cat and I are quite alike, these winter nights:
I consult thesauruses; he forages for mice.
He prowls the darkest corners, while I throw the dice
Of rhyme, and rummage through the OED's delights.

He's all ears and eyes and whiskery antennae
Bristling with the whispered broadcast of the stars,
And I have cruised the ocean of a thousand bars,
And trawled a thousand entries at the dawn of day.

I plucked another goose-quill from the living wing
And opened up my knife, while Cat unsheathed his claws.
Our wild imaginations started to take wing.

We rolled in serendipity upon the mat.
I forged a chapter of the Universal Laws.
Then he became the man, and I became the cat.

1798

I met her in the garden where the poppies grow,
Quite over-canopied with luscious woodbine,
And her cheeks were like roses, or blood dropped on snow;
Her pallid lips were red with Papal Spanish wine.

Lulled in these wild flowers, with dance and delight,
I took my opportunity, and grasped her hand.
She then disclosed the eyelids of her second sight,
And prophesied that I'd forsake my native land.

Before I could protest, she put her mouth to mine
And sucked the broken English from my Gaelic tongue.
She wound me in her briary arms of eglantine.

Two centuries have gone, yet she and I abide
Like emblems of a rebel song no longer sung,
Or snowy blossoms drifting down the mountainside.

1998

In this ceremony, the President will eat the host,
Which represents the transubstantiated moon.
Then Her Nibs'll christen the Montgolfier balloon:
Traditionally, it's always called *The Holy Ghost*.

She steps on board the gondola, and borne high
Above the madding crowd, she showers them with beads
Of mistletoe and amber, opium poppy seeds,
And little petalled parasols of madder dye.

Then all of us imbibe the haemoglobin wine
In dribbled sips of intravenous sacrament,
Where we combine in knowing what is yours is mine.

This is why we can commune so easily, I think:
Already, you've partaken of our President.
You ate her bread. You licked her salt. You drank her drink.

Saké

The female puppet is legless. To make her walk
You must manipulate the hem of her garment.
Her hair is black as night, her face white as chalk.
Beware: she can turn suddenly violent.

When she is not active you must rest her on her stand.
Don't even think of throwing her down on the bed,
For you're the tool, and she the doppelganger hand.
To know her inner self will stand you in good stead.

Let the orbit of her eye accommodate you;
Put yourself between her poppy lips to make her speak;
Let her every practised action be your début.

For once I knew a character like you, my friend,
Who took his puppet drinking seven days a week.
A fortnight past, she took control. You know the end.

Digitalis

Since I got my fingers stuck in a Witch's Glove
One night, my writing hasn't been the same, I fear;
And something's always whispering within my ear
About the murky underworld of goblin love.

That's when Mr Stump takes over – he who writes these lines
In automatic carabine – and I succumb
To all his left-hand fantasies of fife and drum,
Where soldiers sometimes use their guns as concubines.

Or often he describes a land across the sea,
Where all the men are uniformed in sailor blue –
His conversation's like the stumbling of a bee

Within a Fairy's Thimble – blushful Hippocrene –
And then he starts this cuckoo's rumour about you:
That's when I clamp him in my paper-guillotine.

Sayers, or, Both Saw Wonders

We lay down in the Forest of Forget-me-not;
You slept, and from your open lips an Admiral
Emerged as if out for a daily ramble,
Quivering its wings as vivid as a Rorschach blot.

It crept down you, over a stream and through the rye
Into an open socket of an equine skull,
To wander for a lull within that Trojan hull,
Before it crawled out from the other empty eye.

Then it returned into your mouth the way it went.
You woke, and told me of your labyrinthine dream:
The highway – river – palace – rooms of vast extent –

'It looks as if the soul's a butterfly', I said,
'Yet many who've elaborated on this theme
Have never seen the inside of a horse's head.'

Crack

This Fortnight Market last, I fell in with these Keogh boys,
Who plied me liberally with brandywine and snuff.
They showed me upstairs and took off my corduroys,
And dressed me in a raffish crinoline and ruff.

Next they walked me downstairs to their Captain's wake.
He lay trussed in his shanavest and caravat,
His sword and blunderbuss beside. He looked like William Blake.
Thirteen candles signified the sabbat.

The Locals then produced a rock of crystallite,
And short clay pipes, and crumbled leaves of Widow's Weed,
With which we chased the burning tiger through the night.

Come dawn, they asked me to fulfil my woman's role.
I breathed smoke into him, and said the Backwards Creed.
His eyes sprang open, and I saw his very soul.

Twelfth Day

Drunk as a bee that bumbles from deep in the bell
Of a Fairy's Thimble, in a heat-dazed summer meadow,
We sprawled as if we listened to a radio
Which broadcast nothing except insect decibel.

The volume of the field was many atmospheres
Of crawling, chittering, tiny Arcadians,
To whom teeming minutes might be days; and hours years.
In this vast universe, we were the aliens.

Every flower we saw, each stalk, was colonized
By troops of little fellows marching up and down
In perfect harmony, as if transistorized.

I went to pinch one 'twixt my index and my thumb,
When someone turned the volume up in Portadown,
And then I heard the whole field pulsing like an Orange drum.

The Ay O'Haitch

We march the road like regular quaternions
In jackets of the froggy green, and Paddy hats.
Our socks are gartered and our hair in Croppy plaits:
We are the Ancient Order of Hibernians.

Our silken banners waver in the dewy breeze
With emblematic gold embroidery of Ireland:
Wolfhound, Shamrock, Harp, the Plough in Hyades –
Five provinces not fingered by a severed hand.

We blow a fife tune on our red accordions,
And thrum the goatskins of our borrowed Lambeg drums,
For we're the Noble Order of Hibernians.

We are pedestrians, we're not equestrians;
We will outbreed the others; we have done our sums.
Will you, Sir, join our Union of Hibernians?

The Londonderry Air

Snow falls eternally within my souvenir
Of him, who wore the suit of Lincoln corduroy.
He was my noble pikeman, and my pioneer;
Snow falls eternally upon my Danny Boy.

I used to see him at the rising of the moon
With other fellows, exercising in the field,
For they'd refused to take the Saxon gold doubloon –
Indomitable hearts of steel, who'd never yield!

One Sunday, coming home from Mass, from him I stole
A kiss; he left on Monday for to join the war;
I never saw him more, yet he resides within my soul

Like some strange seedling of the plant of Liberty,
That breeds eternally beneath the Northern Star,
Returning as the blossom on the whitethorn tree.

Fear

I fear the vast dimensions of eternity.
I fear the gap between the platform and the train.
I fear the onset of a murderous campaign.
I fear the palpitations caused by too much tea.

I fear the drawn pistol of a rapparee.
I fear the books will not survive the acid rain.
I fear the ruler and the blackboard and the cane.
I fear the Jabberwock, whatever it might be.

I fear the bad decisions of a referee.
I fear the only recourse is to plead insane.
I fear the implications of a lawyer's fee.

I fear the gremlins that have colonized my brain.
I fear to read the small print of the guarantee.
And what else do I fear? Let me begin again.

Fuji Film

I feared the yen was starting to decline again,
Devaluing my take-home honorarium.
I joined the crowd that swarmed beneath the acid rain
Like schools of fishes in a vast aquarium.

Some wore sharkskin suits that shimmered like a rainbow;
Some were surgeons, with a white mask where their mouth
      should be;
Some bore barracuda grins, and some wore minnow;
One fat businessman swam like a manatee.

I saw two lobster samurai produce their swords
Of infinitely hammered folded Zeno steel,
That glittered like the icy blue of Northern fjords.

I snapped them slashing floating dollar bills in half
Beneath the signs for Coke, the giant neon roulette wheel,
The money index pulsing like a cardiograph.

Picador

We swept through Austerlitz and Friedland like a plough
Through bloodied water, and all Europe cowered.
But when we came to Moscow, we were overpowered
By snow; our horses wallowed in the wintry slough.

Up to the stirrups in it, they plunged this way and that,
Slowly scattering across the moonlit landscape.
The Cossack dogs snapped at our heels. We'd no escape.
The huge stars glittered in their frozen concordat.

We found ourselves alone on the edge of a wood,
My horse and I, where wolves howled like a hundred banshees.
My bullets were all spent. I had no food.

I carved the horse's belly open and I crawled
Inside. I ate her flesh for weeks, expiring by degrees.
Some day you'll find us where her bones and mine are sprawled.

Mustard

Populated by poppies, these fields of '14.
The dreams of warriors blow through the summer grass.
Remember the dead by this pane of stained glass.
The bluebells represent their lips of cyanine.

The statues of the saints are draped at Passiontide.
Please take the transubstantiated wine and bread.
The drunken soldiery had taken to the bed.
You'll get a whiff of ethylene and sulphur chloride.

Then came the Angels, with their flaming swords of light.
Church bells doomed and gonged above the town of Mons.
The Tommies rallied, and the Huns were put to flight.

Do you want to try the demonstration gas-mask?
The campaign included many oxymorons.
You want to know how many yards we gained? Don't ask.

The Display Case

Last night Hibernia appeared to me in regal frame,
In Creggan churchyard where I lay near dead from drink.
'Take down these words', she said, 'that all might know my
    claim.'
I opened up a vein and drew my blood for ink –

I'd no accoutrements of writing, save the knife;
The pen she gave me was a feather from her plumage,
And my arm the parchment where I'd sign away my life.
'You seem', she says, 'to have a problem with the language,

'Since you've abandoned it for lisping English,
Scribbling poems in it exclusively, or so I'm told.
Turncoat interpreter, you wonder why I languish?'

Her full speech is tattooed for all time on my mummied arm,
A relic some girl salvaged from the scaffold
Where they quartered me. *God keep the Irish from all harm!*

The Groves of Blarney

If you ever go across the sea to Ireland,
You'll find they speak a language that you do not know,
And all their time's a grand divertimento,
Dancing jigs and reels to McNamara's Band.

'Tis there you'll find the woods of shamrock and shillelagh.
And the pratie gardens full of Easter snow;
You'll hear the blackbird sing a gay risorgimento,
And see Venus rising at the dawning of the day.

Here they'll feed you hot mugs of buttered poteen,
Salty rashers, gander eggs, and soda bread,
And funny cutty pipes of blissful nicotine.

You'll find you will succumb to their endearing charms,
For sometimes they cohabit with the living dead,
And often wake in strange beds, and another's arms.

Banners

For all that died from shot and sword, more died of disease:
Plagues, dysentery, miasmas, suppurating grot
Beyond the non-existent doctors' expertise.
Some were given military burials, others not.

Starved with cold, *La Grande Armee*, like dots in domino,
Stumbled through Borovsk and Vereya to Mojaisk,
To recross the battlefield of Borodino:
For this enormous freezing tomb, no obelisk,

But the ground ploughed by cannonballs, harrowed by lances,
Littered with cuirasses, wheels, rags, and thirty thousand
Bodies with no eyes who devoured our glances.

As we passed them, we almost took them for our foes,
And for a moment I thought of dear old Ireland:
Fields of corpses plentiful as dug potatoes.

Spraying the Potatoes

Knapsack-sprayer on my back, I marched the drills
Of blossoming potatoes – Kerr's Pinks in a frivelled blue,
The Arran Banners wearing white. July was due,
A haze of copper sulphate on the far-off hills.

The bronze noon air was drowsy, unguent as glue.
As I bent over the big oil-drum for a refill,
I heard the axle-roll of a rut-locked tumbril.
It might have come from God-knows-where, or out of the blue.

A verdant man was cuffed and shackled to its bed.
Fourteen troopers rode beside, all dressed in red.
It took them a minute to string him up from the oak tree.

I watched him swing in his Derry green for hours and hours,
His popping eyes of apoplectic liberty
That blindly scanned the blue and white potato flowers.

Heart of Oak

Coming to in the Twelfth Meadow, I was still
Woozy with whatever it was had happened me.
I felt like Ahab's Herman Melville,
Regurgitated by a monster of cetacean pedigree.

It'd seemed I'd swum into my own enormous maw
Some months ago. I'd made the rib-cage my abode:
Vaulted hall wherein a swallowed galleon creaked and yawed,
And labyrinths of gloomy light were blue as woad.

In this realm, everything was fitted to my needs:
The Captain's library, his map and compasses,
His davenport, at which I wrote these many screeds,

His microscope, his grand *pianoforte* –
Only the guns and shot were completely useless.
I left them there to rust when I regained my liberty.

Envoy

Now you've travelled through the Land of Nod and Wink,
And sucked the pap of *papaver somniferum*,
In fields abounding in high cockelorum,
You'll find that everything is slightly out of synch.

These words the ink is written in are not indelible
And every fairy story has its variorum;
For there are many shades of pigment in the spectrum,
And the printed news is always unreliable.

Of maidens, soldiers, presidents and plants I've sung;
Of fairies, fishes, horses, and of headless men;
Of beings from the lowest to the highest rung –

With their long ladder propped against the gates of Heaven,
They're queued up to be rewarded for their grand endeavour,
And receive their campaign haloes on the Twelfth of Never.